# Elderchild

Marlene Fabian Stiles

Published by Marlene Fabian Stiles, 2021.

ELDERCHILD

**First edition. August 6, 2021.**



ISBN: 979-8201594503

Written by Marlene Fabian Stiles.

# Chapter 1 A DAY IN MAY

CHECK MY PULSE. YEP, still have one. All systems go. Now for coffee . . . can't start the day without my morning Joe. Pour icy water into the coffee pot, open the canister.

What's this note? Buy coffee? My heart sinks way down to the toes of my fuzzy house shoes. Damnit, should have put this note someplace where I could see it.

OK, I've got this. Just need to throw on some clothes, sling my purse over my shoulder, throw open the garage door. My car—it's gone!

Is it in the driveway? No such luck. In front of the house? Nope, don't see it. My heart pitter patters. Shield my eyes from the sun, peer up and down the street.

Don't need that cup of coffee anymore. A stiff drink would do me better. Harry will never know if a nip is missing from his stash of hooch. Got to pour myself a tall one before asking my daughter Melissa to notify the police.

"Just handle it yourself, Rhea," my inner voice blurbs. Right! Why listen to Melissa ping on me for leaving the garage door open or forgetting to tell her I'm out of coffee.

After making the call, I'm afraid to gulp down a drink on an empty stomach so I piddle around on pins and needles, waiting for a policeman to show up. They send a clean shaven officer who looks like he just graduated from high school.

When he asks for details, poor pitiful me wrings my hands, shifting my weight from one shoe to the other. "Don't understand how this happened. I locked three out of the four doors."

The much-too-young officer seems to smirk as he says, "Yep, that fourth door will do it every time." His drawl is totally deadpan but there's chuckle in his voice. Of all the nerve! Look at me—eighty something years old, a damsel in distress and he's got the nerve to laugh.

He keeps grilling me like I'm a witness on *Law and Order*. "Do you remember the last time you drove your car?"

"Uhm . . . yesterday." Think it was yesterday. Days tend to smear together. "Maybe it was the day before."

"Do you know where you were going?"

"Don't go anywhere." Except shopping.

"Is there anyone who might have borrowed your car?"

"No, my daughter Melissa has her own car and my husband does, too." Think he does.

The policeman takes notes. He doesn't even look at me as he repeats my name.

"So . . . Rhea Laska . . . do you have your car's registration?"

"Of course." Mutter under my breath, "I'm not a nincompoop." Oh damn, where is it? Somewhere in my purse under all this junk. Kleenex . . . wrinkled receipts . . . five tubes of lipstick and only need one.

After a few minutes the young policeman asks, "Isn't that your wallet?"

"Uh . . . yes, thank you." Let him search it. "You should have no trouble finding my car. It's red."

Same poker face but there's a twitter in his voice. "We'll do our best, ma'am."

That's not good enough! "You've got to find it! It's not some beat-up old jalopy—"

His face goes blank. "A what?"

"Jalopy. That's a term for an old car." One last play for sympathy. "My daughter Melissa will have a hissy fit if she finds out it's gone." She's already bellyaching about all the things she has to do for me.

With youthful confidence the police officer hands me his card and says, "We'll be in touch." Then he pretends to answer another call but he's probably making an excuse to leave. The door swings shut behind him so fast it nearly smacks him in the derriere.

Grumble to my hubby Harry, "He's not going to find it. Bet he can't even find the catsup bottle in the refrigerator." Harry can't find the catsup either so he doesn't say anything.

What's the number on this card? The letters blur together like a water stain. Need to borrow Harry's reading glasses—

No, better hide the card first. If Melissa sees it, she'll make a big deal out of me losing the car even though she wants me to get rid of things. She's always harping about how we should sell this house and move into assisted living. Then we can use the equity to have someone else take care of us. But assisted living costs a lot and what if we run out of money before we die? Can't think about that now. It's too scary,

"Nothing works in an old house except the owner," that's what Harry likes to say. True, the house takes a lot of upkeep and Melissa says we need to sell it while the real estate market's hot. Only we don't want to move.

The card begs for my attention. Where to hide it? Not near the picture window, that's for sure . . . too much sunshine washing through the glass, showing off the smudges. Just stuff it under a pile of magazines. "Honestly, Harry, we've been in this house nearly fifty years. What would we do with all this junk? Half of it's yours, you know."

Harry doesn't say anything. He's probably holed up in his corner, buried under a newspaper in that beat-up Lazy-boy chair he won't throw out even though it doesn't match the French Provincial furniture we bought on sale for our fortieth anniversary.

"Harry?"

Still no answer.

Oh, right: Harry's dead. He has been dead for two years now . . . or is it three? Plop into my brocaded armchair, count backwards from the most recent photographs plastering the wall, trying to make sense of time. It streams past me in a waltz of seasons: daffy-down-dilly spring decked out in green and yellow, summer lazing in dog day heat, autumn regal and russet, white-boned winter. Four long seasons form a rainbow arch from my childhood to the present, everything else is quite literally water under the bridge. Dunno where the years went.

"They keep unraveling like loose threads." Heavens to Murgatroyd, I'm talking to myself.

Run my finger along the edge of Harry's last picture, dislodge a fleck of dust and follow its trail for a millisecond as it hitches a ride on a sunbeam then disappears.

Pride myself on being an immaculate housekeeper but forgot to dust the pictures. Drat that sunshine, highlighting all that ashy powder on the frames. Days don't seem to stretch like they used to . . . no sooner does the sun come up than it's time for lunch. After watching my soap opera, shadows eat up the leftover afternoon.

Maybe we *should* go into assisted living, getting tired of fighting dust bunnies single handedly. Wipe my fingertips, turn to Harry.

"What do you think? Shall we give assisted living a try?"

Harry's chair is empty.

He's probably out in the garage, fooling around with a broken gadget.

That's precisely why we can't move. What would Harry do with all his tools? For that matter, what would happen to my collection of hand-painted teapots? Melissa doesn't want them and Dawn . . .

Dawn moved to California to get away from me.

Fiddlesticks! Have a headache now. Just thinking about downsizing after five decades under one roof is like climbing Mount Everest. Time for a nap. Who covered Harry's chair with a sheet? Oh, it's just a shadow. Nestle into his Lazy-Boy chair. The musky smell of his aftershave is still embedded in the upholstery. Love that man!

Think I'll shut my eyes for just a minute . . .

Wake up to twilit blight. Shadows smother the sun in a shroud of gray silk. Everything is distorted—like the world's plunged underwater.

My voice cracks. "Where am I?" No one's around. Jittering nerves pinch my gut. Stomach feels queasy like it did on the day Petey the bratty boy across the street put his parents' car into reverse and rammed it into our fence. I'm playing with my big sister Selina in the front yard. We run inside our house, crying for Mama.

"Now Sissy," Mamma tells Selina, "It's alright, a fence can be mended."

Sissy is a carbon copy of Mama with sloe black eyes and thick, wavy hair. When they both smile, the sun breaks through the clouds and everything feels pleasant and warm again.

Will everything be alright now? Can still smell reeking rubber, hear tires screech through the crack of splintered wood. We go to the window and stare as Petey bolts from his parents' car and runs down the street. For an instant he's more alive than my colorless living room drenched in shadow.

Switching on the light I'm shocked to find my fingers are twisted, blotted with age spots. These look like Grandma's hands, but that's not possible . . . I'm seven years old and that brat across the street just crashed a car into our fence.

Two middle-aged women in the photographs smile mysteriously like they're hiding something. The one with dark hair looks familiar. Didn't she scold me the other day for turning a corner too fast and hitting a curb? Don't understand why she's upset. We have insurance.

Also have a bad feeling that's the same dark-haired woman who keeps barging into my house, asking "do you need anything?" and stuffing my freezer full of food packages. She looks frazzled all the time so I'm sure she'll be mad when she finds out my car is lost. Can hear her raving now, "You need to stop driving, Mom."

Might as well 'fess up. Don't really want to, but Mama's voice plays like a broken record in my head, "Never put off tomorrow what you can do today."

Okay, just get this over with. Only . . . dunno which button to push on the phone so try number one. "Bingo!" A voice that sounds a lot like my daughter Melissa tells me to leave a message.

Good! Didn't really want to talk to her anyway.

Another voice interrupts me. "Mom, are you okay?"

Holy Moley, she knows I'm hiding something! Still don't want to tell her my car's been stolen. Bite my lip, play for time. Maybe the police will find it.

Put on a sunshiny voice. "Just calling to say hello." Hope she doesn't know I'm lying.

Melissa talks nonsense. "Don't forget to turn the thermostat up. It's supposed to be cold tonight."

"Is it going to freeze?"

"Not on the first of May."

"We've had freezes in May. Mama's garden froze the year when that neighbor boy drove his parents' car into our fence."

"What are you talking about?"

Clear my throat. "What I mean to say is—" That always buys me time to think.

"Did you get any nibbles on your website?"

"I don't have a website," Melissa says.

"That thing you put on the internet."

"Mike's grill? It sold on Craig's list eons ago."

"So that's why he divorced you." Wait for her to say something. Silence. "What I mean to say is—what happened with that advertisement you placed for a date?"

That hits a nerve. Melissa sucks in her breath. "It's not an advertisement, Mom. I joined a meet-up group."

Should do that, too. "Your father's giving me the silent treatment." Lower my voice so Harry can't hear. "He's having an affair."

Harry's the tall, handsome, silent type but he's been much too quiet lately. For years now we don't say much of anything except "Pass the salt" or "Which section of the paper do you want?" Lately the silence seems to be taking on a life of its own.

Melissa clams up for a moment then blurts, "Daddy's dead, Mom." She sounds upset. "I've got another call coming in."

"You get more phone calls than Carter's got liver pills."

After we hang up, the pictures on the wall leer like memories frozen in time. There's Sissy with Mama and Papa and me posing on our front porch and an old time wedding photo of a bride in a dress that's out of date. Here's a young couple with two kids, then lots of school pictures of those same little girls with braces glittering their teeth and more wedding photos. These women look vaguely familiar but who is that old couple smiling at the camera like they're sharing a guilty secret?

Shadows nibble at the edges of the photographs like hungry mice. Gasp! That's Harry and me on a Caribbean cruise to celebrate our fiftieth wedding anniversary. Jumping Jehoshaphat! My hair looks like a rat's nest. Need to dye it and wear it in curls like in my wedding portrait.

I'm so pretty in that flouncy dress. All the bridal gowns that season were form-fitting satin but mine has a full skirt with tiered ruffles like Vivian Leigh wore in *Gone with the Wind*. Mama had a conniption fit when she saw the scooped neckline. She insisted on me wearing a high-necked, long-sleeved blouse underneath so we wouldn't get thrown out of church.

Giggle. Just imagine the headlines— "Bride banished on her wedding day."

My wedding dress was downright modest compared to my daughter Dawn's. Hers was so tight, she was practically falling out of it. Low back, spaghetti straps—nothing left to the imagination. She looked like a street walker. Too bad she didn't slim down twenty pounds before she took that picture.

Reach up to straighten the crooked frame, that's when the darn phone rings. It's Melissa calling to apologize for putting me on hold. "What were we talking about?"

"Dunno. You called me."

"You called me first."

"No, you called me."

This conversation is turning into a replay of Abbott and Costello's *Who's on First*. "Smell something burning." Hang up fast. Uh-oh, not a good idea. Anything burning throws Melissa into a panic. Now she'll probably drive over to make sure my house isn't on fire.

Redial, get her voicemail. "Nothing's burning." Slam down the receiver so she can't ask any more questions. Yesterday forgot and left a skillet on the stove, went outside to get the newspaper, stopped to pull some dandelions strangling my grape hyacinth. Smoke billowed out the kitchen window. Drop everything, rush inside and find little yellow flames hopping around the stovetop like manic demons.

Pull the sprayer from the sink, water the fire until it goes out. The smoke alarm won't shut off and blisters my ears. Have to knock it off the wall with a broom and take out the batteries.

Melissa calls back. "Mom, don't bother turning on the stove."

Heavens to Betsy, she knows! Better confess but she prattles first, "The freezer's packed with dinners. Just pop one in the microwave. All you have to do is push the reheat button."

The tiny hairs on the nape of my neck bristle. "You don't have to tell me how to do every little thing. I'm not helpless."

"Yesterday you didn't remember how to use your microwave. I had to drive over and show you."

Here we go again. Every time she has to drive across town she acts like I'm on the dark side of the moon.

Melissa keeps nagging. "This time throw the leftovers away. Don't wad a roll of cellophane around them and stick them back in the freezer. We just have to toss them out before they turn into a biology experiment."

I'm mortified. "There's a depression going on. Mama says you shouldn't waste food.

"The servings aren't that large, Mom. You need to be part of the clean plate club."

That sounds like something Mama would say.

"You give me too many vegetables."

Melissa gets real quiet then says, "Be sure to turn the heat up. It'll be chilly tonight."

"Good point. Gotta go. If it's that cold, better bring my basket of wisteria inside."

Melissa's voice rings in my ears, "Why are you bothering, Mom? Those are silk flowers."

"Right." Can't garden anymore and if the wisteria's left outside, all the neighbors will know it.

# Chapter 2 LATER THE SAME DAY

A VOICE RATTLES IN my head. "Don't climb up on that porch swing!" Is that Melissa or Mama?

Sissy giggles as we cling to the chains like a couple of monkeys. When Mama scolds us, we clamber down and sit on the swing as prim as little angels. The minute she goes back in the house, Sissy pokes me. In no time at all we're climbing like monkeys again.

This time it's different. I'm not ignoring Mama, just have to take my basket of silk wisteria back into the house before it freezes tonight. It's too hard to drag a chair onto the porch and the swing is handy even if it's swaying like crazy.

I climb up . . . hang tight . . . just a little further now . . .

Dang! The swing is wobbling, making me lose my balance. Grab onto the chain, cling to it for dear life so I don't fall. Drat that wind! It keeps knocking the basket around. Grandpa would call this a williwaw. He likes funny sounding words like loblolly for mud and collywobbles for intestinal distress. Got collywobbles all right, but have to get my wisteria inside while there's still daylight so the neighbors won't know my thumb isn't green anymore.

For years my yard was the nicest on my block. All through the winter geranium cuttings flourished on my windowsill, ready for the porch box each spring. Now I'm fussing over a basket of silk flowers. Melissa's right, just let it go.

No, guldarnit! I'm getting that basket down if it's the last thing—

Sweet Mother of Mercy!

The ground flies up, slaps me hard and cracks my head like an egg. Something warm trickles into my eyes. Blood?

Roll onto my hip . . . Holy cow! It hurts something awful to crouch on my bony knees. Mighty heave, grapple the porch rail, crawl back onto my feet.

At least the wisteria basket's on the ground. Snatch it up and go inside.

Better not get blood on the carpet. Melissa will be mad for sure. Head for the bathroom, wash my face to hide the evidence. Lord Almighty, Lady Macbeth was right. Who would have thought there could be so much blood?

It's slippery, too. The bandages won't stick to my forehead. A whole box later they're still flaking off. Just wrap a roll of gauze around my head like Boris Karloff did in *The Mummy*.

Better find a turban to cover this up. Rummage through my closet . . . all I have are mismatched shoes. Where are my hat boxes? Dozens of hats with color-coordinated gloves and not one in sight. They must have disappeared into the same black hole that swallowed my car.

Finally find a turban inside a Samsonite suitcase. It covers my bandages and makes me look like an old-time movie star.

Uh-oh—huge, black bruise on my arm. Pull on a sweater. Problem solved. Melissa can't say anything, she knows there's a cold spell.

Now to wash the blood off the wisteria blossoms. The less Melissa knows the better.

# Chapter 3 THE DAY AFTER THE DAY BEFORE

WHAT'S WRONG WITH ME? The wisteria is sitting in plain sight on the coffee table. I'm sweating bullets as I stuff it into a garbage bag and stash it in my closet for safekeeping. Got all twitterpated for nothing. When Melissa comes over after work, she doesn't even notice that I'm wearing a turban and sweater.

Instead she says, "Sorry I can't stay long."

What a relief. "That's alright." Pretend to wipe away a tear.

"It's just that I have a coffee date—"

"Alright. See you later, alligator."

Putting her hands on her hips, she morphs into a pouty little girl. "Don't be like that, Mom."

"Like what?" Just save my breath. She talks about how much she does for me and how little it's appreciated. This middle-aged woman doesn't match that framed picture of my precious little girl in a Swiss polka-dot dress, smiling for the camera.

She finally goes home. Now to enjoy some peace and quiet. The phone rings, jarring my nerves with its incessant demand to be answered.

Not in the mood to talk, tuck it under a pillow.

It keeps ringing. Eventually the answering machine belches out an official sounding voice, "This message is for Rhea Laska. The police located your car abandoned in the parking lot at the North Gate Shopping Mall—"

That's right! Drove to the mall the day before my car went missing. Must have forgotten and taken the bus home.

Dig through the pillows on the couch, uncover the phone. It blinks at me angrily, demanding a return call to thank the police for finding my car and to apologize for presuming it was stolen. It's a simple mistake anyone could make.

Now just need a ride to the mall to pick my car up. The phone must know that, too. It rings in my hand.

"Mom, this is Melissa. Please don't be angry with me—"

"Angry? I'm ecstatic. The police found my car. Can you give me a ride to the North Gate Mall?"

"What are you talking about?"

"My car. It was lost, now it's found."

Instead of being happy for me, Melissa sounds more upset than ever. "Mom, why didn't you tell me your car was missing?"

"I'm telling you now. Can you give me a ride?"

Her sigh echoes through the phone. "Sure wish you had said something earlier. You know I have a coffee date this evening."

"Great! Did someone answer your advertisement?"

"It wasn't an advertisement."

"Is he nice?"

"We chatted on-line and decided to meet in person."

"If he makes you pay for the coffee, dump him. Don't marry a cheapskate."

"I'm not marrying him, Mom. We're just meeting up."

"Why bother if you're not going to marry him?"

Melissa is silent, but only for a moment. "We just want to get to know each other better." She belts out a martyr's sigh. "Look, I'll take you to the mall before work tomorrow morning. Can you be ready by eight-thirty?"

"Of course. Have to get up early to make you girls breakfast."

"That was when we were in school, Mom."

"What I mean to say is—no point in spending all day in bed lollygagging." Grandpa liked that word, too.

"All right. I'll see you in the morning."

"I'll be waiting."

"Please be ready. I'm not going to have a lot of time."

Melissa never has time. Should probably get her a bottle of thyme for her birthday since she keeps running out.

# Chapter 4 THE CRASH

MELISSA SOUNDS HURT, even a little angry when she intrudes on my dreams. "Mom, wake up! You promised to be ready by eight thirty."

"I'm ready, just waiting for you." What luck, forgot to undress when I fell asleep last night.

She puts her hands on her hips. "I tried to call but your phone is off the hook—again."

So that's what's buzzing! Thought it was Harry's electric razor. Shuffle into my shoes. "Was just shutting my eyes for a minute, waiting for you." Pause at the mirror to adjust my turban and fluff out my sweater. "There. I'm all hunky dory."

Melissa checks her watch. "Let's get going, Mom. I've got to be at work by nine."

She looks hassled. Probably shouldn't have bothered her. "Never mind, I'll get Harry to drive me." Now where is that man when you need him? "Harry!" My shout echoes down the hallway. "He's probably fooling around in the garage, fixing some contraption."

Melissa's voice drops. "Daddy passed away, Mom."

"If you say so." Melissa's such a pigheaded little girl, there's no reasoning with her. She gets her stubborn streak from Harry, not from me. She's a carbon copy of that man, always carrying on about money and how we need to save more than we spend or we'll never be able to retire. Worse yet, we'll be forced into one of those cut-rate nursing homes and have to live on charity.

We drive in silence to the North Gate Mall. The parking lot is nearly empty so we have no trouble spotting my car.

Melissa checks her watch then says, "I don't feel good about you driving, but I might lose my job if I'm late for work again. I'll call you tonight after I get home."

She leaves me next to my car and drives off. Didn't get to ask if her meet-up date paid for coffee or if he turned out to be a cheapskate.

Oh well, don't have to hurry anymore. Have my car, have my keys. Maybe I'll get a cup of cappuccino before driving home. But the mall is locked up tight as a drum. The sign says they open at ten. That seems like a long time to wait. Might as well go home and make my own cup of coffee. Cheaper that way.

Well this is a fine kettle of fish! Had my car keys a minute ago but now they're gone. Dump everything out of my purse onto the hood of the car. A sneaky little wind snatches up my wads of Kleenex and whisks them away.

Before the wind grabs anything else, shove my wallet, brush, comb, lipstick, compact, pens, notebook and breath mints back in my purse. Now where are my keys? Dump everything out again—there they are at the bottom.

Finally! The car door opens.

If this doesn't beat all! Got my car back and now the engine won't start. "You son of a beast!" That's Harry's expletive. It always works for him but the car ignores me. Maybe if the key turns a little more to the right . . .

Gears grind like fingernails dragging across a chalkboard but the car sputters to life and lurches forward. On my way!

Car has a mind of its own as it zips around one corner after another, negotiating a maze of streets that don't look at all familiar. Is the mall this close to the cemetery? Since I'm here, might as well check on those plots Harry bought years ago to see if he really did pass away.

My sixth sense tells me Melissa is covering for him so I don't catch him with his girlfriend. She's Daddy's girl—always has been ever since she was knee high to a grasshopper. If Harry ran off with another woman, she'd never tell me.

That must be why Melissa is so touchy these days, she doesn't want to give up Harry's secrets. Or maybe she's still upset about me giving my credit card number to that pesky lady on the phone. Melissa canceled my card and cut it up. Jeepers! Only gave it to the pesky lady so she'd stop pestering me.

Why is Melissa so mean to me all the time? My sigh filters down to the soles of my shoes. It thumps the gas pedal like a lead weight as the car turns into the cemetery . . .

Jumping Jehoshaphat! Car bolts forward like a runaway racehorse. "Stop!" Car won't listen. It just zooms faster. Cling to the steering wheel and pray to every saint in heaven—

Lord have mercy! An oak tree jumps out of its roots and thumps down right out in front of me.

Tree bark splinters.

Glass shatters.

Metal crunches.

A billowy cloud suffocates me in its feathery pillow.

Release my grip on the wheel. The world goes black.

# Chapter 5 THE AFTERMATH

WAKE UP MUMBLING, "WHAT happened?"

Open my eyes, close them, open them again. A fuzzy mist slides away as a young man with shiny hair and dreamy eyes bends over me. Maybe I'm in heaven—he's as handsome as an angel.

"Ma'am?" he asks in a polite tone of voice. "What's your name?"

Gee whillikers, if he's an angel, he ought to know that. Maybe this is a test. "Rhea Brookshire—no, Laska," My mouth hurts too much to smile. That's strange. Didn't think you felt anything once you were dead.

The young man keeps asking the most curious questions. "Do you know what day it is?"

His eyes are the exact color of bluebells.

Have to get this right. "Thursday—no, it's Wednesday." He looks concerned. Must have failed the test.

Now he says something stupid. "Do you know who the president is?"

Mama says it's rude to talk about religion and politics. "Humph. Does it matter?"

"You may have a concussion, ma'am. We're taking you to the hospital."

That's nice of him. "Can you take me home instead?"

"You really should get checked out at a hospital, ma'am." He's such a pleasant young man and a good conversationalist. He and another fellow who isn't nearly as good-looking lift me into an ambulance.

Melissa will be green with envy when she learns I've met a nice-looking young man and didn't even have to join a meet-up group!

# Chapter 6 JUST ANOTHER DAY

MELISSA IS SO LIVID, I'm afraid she'll implode. "Mom, you could have killed yourself!"

That's what Mama says when Sissy climbs out of the attic window and onto our roof. But nothing ever happens.

Won't give Melissa the satisfaction of admitting she's right, not for all the tea in China. Turn to a high school student who's pretending to be a doctor, hoping he'll back me up. But he's obsessing about an egg-size bump on the back of my head. "This isn't an injury she could receive from an airbag."

Melissa's eyes drill through me. "What else happened, Mom?"

"Dunno." That's my stock answer so people will leave me alone and stop annoying me.

Melissa is relentless. "Try to remember." It seems even the teenage doctor is glowering at me.

Mumble about the cold and the neighbors and my basket of wisteria, give them a few crumbs of information and let them fit the jigsaw pieces together. Fold my arms and hunker down, wish they'd stare at somebody else.

They talk about me like I'm not in the room. The doctor grumps, "There's a lot of blood built up under her skin. If the bruise had been iced right away, it would have kept the swelling down."

Melissa keeps saying she doesn't know what happened. "I check on her every single day."

Close my eyes, let them jibber-jabber. Open my eyes, can't take it anymore. "Let's go home, Melissa." They still ignore me.

Slide off the cot and barge out into a long corridor partitioned by curtains. Dunno how to get out of here and have to go back to Melissa with my tail between my legs.

First we wait to be released and that takes forever. Melisa hangs onto my hand like I'm a four-year-old who might wander off as she ushers me down the hallway. "This was a wake-up call, Mom. You're lucky you didn't hurt anyone else when your car hit that tree."

"Is the tree OK?"

Melissa brushes a tear from her eye. "A huge branch toppled onto the passenger's side and pancaked your engine. If it had fallen on the driver's side, you wouldn't be here right now."

What does a pancaked engine look like? We wander around the parking lot. "Where's my car?"

Melissa gives me a strange look. "It's totaled, Mom."

"Total what? I'm out of coffee and you don't have time to drive me anywhere."

She could inflate hot air balloons with her sigh. "I'll contact a home health care service to look after you and take you places. It's not cheap, but we can work a few hours a week into your budget. I'll ask Dawn to pitch in, too."

Time to dig in my heels. "Don't want a bunch of strangers tromping around my house."

"Mom, I can't keep taking time off work."

"So don't." By now I'm starting to feel light-headed from all this arguing. That probably means my blood pressure reached its boiling point.

Melissa doesn't notice. "Be reasonable, Mom. You need help." She keeps saying that but she's the only one who ever shows up.

"No, you need help. Not me."

She starts to cry. Hate that—it's worse than her lectures.

Try to cheer her up. "I've managed just fine for fifty . . . sixty . . . well for a lot of years."

"You need someone to do light cleaning and run errands. And this time I'm not letting Dawn off the hook. The least she can do is help out with expenses."

"Why are we talking about dawn?" Don't usually get up in time to see the sunrise.

Melissa doesn't make sense. "Dawn thinks she can just come around once in a blue moon—"

"There's a moon?" Scan the blue sky for a wisp of white floating like the Cheshire Cat's smile among the feathery clouds.

Melissa frowns. "We're talking about my sister Dawn."

"Oh." Don't want to drag my absentee daughter into this. She goes crazy when we discuss money, always thinks everything costs too much.

As Melissa drives me home, I cross my arms and ask, "Is this about the dust bunnies under the couch?"

She doesn't answer.

Two can play this game. "Just let me off at the corner grocery."

"You have a concussion, Mom. You need to go home. I'll call you every hour to check on you and come over right after work."

Melissa parks in front of the house. She escorts me inside then gives me a quick peck on the cheek before hurrying back to her car. It's like she can't run away from me fast enough. Maybe she's giving me the slip so she can play with children her own age.

Sissy does that too, 'cause I'm a tag-along little sister.

# Chapter 7 TWO DAYS AFTER THE DAY BEFORE

I GET UP THE GUTS TO cross the street.

Can hear Mama say, "Rhea, you can do this. You're a big girl now." Stop at the corner, look both ways because Mama says to be extra careful about crossing intersections. Sure enough, a car turns around the curb too fast, just missing my foot. Scramble back onto the sidewalk, walk to the corner. I'll cross the street later.

Look for the candy store right next door to a sewing notions shop that has a trained monkey.

The stores aren't here anymore! Gawk around. When did they move it? The houses at this end of my block don't look anything like the ones in my living room window.

A crack in the sidewalk almost trips me up. What does Sissy say? "Step on a crack, break your Mama's back." Take excruciating care to step around all the cracks in the sidewalk until they form a hopscotch pattern. Hop from square to square. Sharp pain shoots up my leg.

The Charlie horse hurts so bad . . . lean against a fence and rub my leg until the cramp goes away. Peer down the street. Looks like there's a bridge at the end of the block, looping the river. Maybe the candy store is on the other side of that bridge.

My shoes are tired and don't want to walk. Have to hobble along, panting for breath. Reach the bridge and look over the railing at the spine-tingling drop. Such a long way down to where the river trickles through thickets of dry reeds that stand up straight like rusty nails.

Grandpa had all kinds of stories about pioneers crossing this river. "They had to keep moving so their wagons didn't get stuck in quicksand." He wasn't lying. "Some of those poor souls went down anyway. No one ever saw hide nor hair of them again."

Back away from the railing, look for the grocery store. Can see it in my mind's eye plain as day . . . the white enamel meat counter and a butcher in his red-stained apron, shelves crowded with cans that reach above my head, the shiny silver and black cash register that dinged every time the butcher's wife rang up a sale.

Sissy and I go next door to the candy store. Sissy likes peppermint but I like licorice.

Look around for Sissy. Where is she anyway? She probably ran off to play with her friends again. Now I'll have to find my way back home all by myself, only none of these houses look familiar.

Sissy's going to be in a lot of trouble for leaving me.

A dusty wind prickles my neck. Step off the curb to get away from the wind. A car honks as it whizzes by.

That was close! Have to cross the street to get home, but more and more cars are zooming past me like they're on a race track. My legs turn to jelly. For one terrifying moment it feels like I'm caught in quicksand.

No, I'm standing on the curb, but something is wrong with my legs. They're thick like elephant trunks and have ugly blue veins bulging out all over.

Running home is like slogging through molasses. Another car honks and then another. A candy wrapper flutters in the wind and whips past my ear.

Made it! "Sissy? You can come out now!" She's nowhere in sight. Must be playing hide and seek, lurking in the juniper bushes.

"Be that way!" Toss my nose in the air and tromp down the street.

Oh this is bad . . . it's not my street. Better find a policeman to help me find my way home. Mama makes me memorize, "My name is Rhea Brookshire. My parents are Mama Lilly and Papa Sam. We live in a red brick house with a rose trellis over the gate." But what if he asks for my house number? Is it three or five?

This street doesn't look right, so keep walking. All the while the wind blows cold and a lavender stain spreads across the gray sky. My knees knock together, drumming a prayer. "Guardian Angel, be my guide. Always walk right by my side. Do not leave me in the night. Keep me safe till morning light."

Angel guides me all the way home.

# Chapter 8 ANOTHER DAY ALONG THE WAY

I JANGLE AN UGLY SILVER chain that Melissa clamps around my wrist. "This is hideous. What happened to my nice jewelry?"

She ignores me and fastens the clasp.

Wiggle wriggle . . . can't slip it off, my wrist is too big. "Hate this!"

Melissa sounds grumpy. "This is an identification bracelet, Mom. You're lucky the neighbors saw you and brought you home when you got lost."

"It looks like one of those rabies tags you hang around a dog's neck."

She has no sympathy. "It's engraved with your name and address, also my phone number in case of an emergency."

Bet she's making me wear this so she and that sister of hers can steal my silver charm bracelet.

"Mom, don't." Melissa stops me from trying to yank the I.D. bracelet over my wrist. When she places her hand over mine, the freckles march all the way up her arm to the tiny sleeve of her snug red dress. Heavens to Betsy, what happened to my pretty little girl with shining eyes the color of roasted peanuts?

"This is for your own good, Mom."

"What are you talking about?" Calm down, stare at the ceiling until she takes the hint and decides to leave. I'll ask Harry to get his pliers and pry this damned thing off . . . if he isn't out with his floozy.

"Mom," the woman in the too-tight red dress chatters, "I shudder to think what could have happened to you."

"Couldn't be worse than getting up on a chair to get a teacup out of the china closet and pulling a whole stack of dishes down on me."

The woman looks alarmed. "When did that happen?"

My eyes shift to the floor. I'm six, maybe seven. Mama is still mad at me.

Lady in Red says, "Just promise me you won't get up on chairs and you won't wander off again."

She's as bossy as Sissy. Close my eyes, open them. She morphs back into my sweet daughter.

Lean closer and squint. Quick as a wink, my baby girl is gone. In her place is a middle-aged woman with salt-and-pepper curls clumped over her head like a swim cap with rubber flowers. "Melissa?"

"Yes, Mom?"

"You ought to dye your hair. You look old."

Her lips tighten into a thin, red line that matches her dress. "Listen to me, Mom. I'm at my wits end. You've got to promise to stay out of trouble. There's no way we can afford to have someone stay here with you 24/7, even if we put a reverse mortgage on the house and Dawn shells out some cash."

What in Sam Hill is she talking about?

"Alright." That shuts her up. Slip my hand into my pocket, cross my fingers. Always do that when Sissy makes me promise not to tag after her.

# Chapter 9 TIME FOR EVERY SEASON

DON'T KNOW WHY MELISSA'S mad at me. Say, "Just hold your horses, I'll be good as gold." Her tight, red lips finally stop frowning.

This is a lot like the time Sissy tells me to melt crayons on the heat register so we can build a wax sculpture. It's all Sissy's fault but Mama scolds me for being a bad girl.

After Melissa leaves, decide to find my family so ramble around the house calling for Mama, Papa and Sissy. Why would they go off without me? Unless . . .

A cold, sick feeling settles in the pit of my stomach. Maybe this is the wrong house! Where's Mama's wicker rocker and the big, overstuffed armchair with the maroon afghan where Papa sits when he reads the evening paper?

This is definitely not my house. It's filled with stiff furniture and photographs papering the walls.

Throw open the front door, step out onto a wide front porch flanked by a shockingly empty flower box. Mama would never stand for that. She always keeps her flower box filled with coleus and red geraniums.

Got to find my way home! The wrought iron railing is icy cold. Have to clamber down the steps one at a time. A sinking feeling tightens inside me like a corkscrew and turns my stomach inside out.

I'm lost and don't know what to do. Old timers like Grandpa say to follow the North Star. But there's no stars out and the too-bright sun bleaches the sky to a powdery blue.

Wander down this street and then another, looking and hoping . . .

Safe at last! There's my school at the end of the block. Joy of joys, hurry to the three story brick building.

Wait a minute, this looks more like a prison. No, it's a school alright. A prison wouldn't have a playground.

Swings! What did Robert Louis Stevenson say? "Go up in the air so blue . . . the most wonderful thing ever a child can do . . ." Love swinging high in the air, brushing my toes against the clouds.

The chains on this swing creak under me. Must have gained a couple of pounds. Kick the dust to get started. Nothing happens. This swing set must be broken. Dangle my feet and look for clouds in the sky until a shadow falls across my path.

"Are you all right, ma'am?" a deep voice asks.

Squint into the sunlight. "Please help me, I'm lost."

The policeman acts concerned. "Where do you live, ma'am?"

Take a deep breath and recite: "My parents are Mama Lilly and Papa Sam."

He keeps asking curious questions. "Is there anyone I can call?"

I show him my bracelet. "This isn't my prettiest one. The others are in my jewelry box."

"Good, there's an emergency contact. Do you live alone?"

"No, with my family. They're supposed to take care of me but they left me and went away." Gulp down my tears. How could they move and leave me behind?

The policeman makes a call and talks to someone. Then he tells me, "I'll take you home now. Your daughter Melissa is going to meet us there."

Maybe he thinks Sissy is my daughter—no that would not make sense.

The kind man takes me home and we meet up with a woman in a red dress who calls herself Melissa. She says she's my daughter. I believe her because she's the spitting image of Harry, but she looks lonely.

Better invite the nice young man to stay for dinner. That way Melissa can stop advertising for dates. Darn it, he declines but maybe that's just as well because he and Melissa do *not* hit it off. She actually seems miffed that I brought a nice young man home to meet her.

"You catch more flies with honey than you do with vinegar." That's what Mama always says. "Never throw brickbats or listen to scuttlebutt."

Melissa sounds a lot like Grandma when she scolds, "You promised not to go wandering, Mom. Are you getting back at me because I didn't take you grocery shopping yesterday?"

"Don't need you to drive me around! Your father can do it."

Melissa dabs at her eyes. "Daddy's not here anymore, Mom."

Darn that Harry. He's never around when I need him. That proves beyond a shadow of a doubt—he *is* having an affair.

# Chapter 10 SOMEWHERE IN TIME

What's wrong with my television? According to the wall clock it's time for my soap opera. Flip through the channels, skim program after program, can't find my story. So many choices and nothing to see.

Can hear Grandpa saying, "Don't let yourself get all twitterpated."

"You're right." Feel stupid, talking to his picture. Can't find my story so might as well go back to bed. Kind of tired anyway. But a doctor—maybe it's a TV actor—reminds me to take one of those little blue pills to help me sleep.

"Common side effects are nausea and diarrhea," the same voice advises me not to take them on an empty stomach.

"Okey dokey." A chocolate chip cookie would taste good, only there aren't any in the refrigerator, just a gallon of ice cream. Sissy isn't around to tattle on me. Eat a whole bowlful then look for our ceramic cookie jar shaped like a pumpkin.

There's a green cookie jar on the counter so the pumpkin must not be ripe. At least it's full of cookies.

"Blech! These are stale!" Mama's oatmeal cookies are always warm and sugary when she takes them out of the oven. These taste like sawdust.

Spit them out and head to the bathroom to rinse my mouth. Lots of bottles in the cabinet.

Two pills are better than one. Choke them down, head down the hallway—

Everything goes wobbly. Feel like Alice in Wonderland falling down a rabbit hole, tumbling down, down . . .

Ouch! Somebody hits their head on the wall. Oh, it's me.

Now I'm in a different hallway that stretches to forever. It's lined with doors on either side and they're all closed tight.

My voice gets small. "Mama?" Nudge a door open. Everything is blinding white. Shiver as I step into freshly fallen snow.

I'm falling face first into a snowbank but this time two strong arms catch me. Mama's brown leather gloves wrap around my pink jumpsuit.

Her voice lilts like a melody. "This is your first snow, baby girl. Go ahead and take a step. I've got you now." Mama holds me upright.

Pain pounds in my head. The snow turns black. Open my eyes, close them, open them again. I'm back in the hallway outside my bedroom.

"Mama?" Pain weighs down my head like an anvil. Crawling on my hands and knees, I reach the nearest door and push it open. Don't recognize this room. "Mama, I'm lost." Tears roll down my cheeks.

Can hear Mama say, "It's all right, baby girl. Go ahead and cry. Tears are angel's kisses."

Wipe my nose with my sleeve and curl into a tight ball, trying to feel Mama's arms wrap around me.

# **Chapter 11 TIME STANDING STILL**

Jeepers' creepers, dance a jig in my sneakers! The mailman delivers an important looking envelope with my name on it.

Wave it triumphantly in my daughter Melissa's face. "Look at this! We're millionaires! That's the third time we won this year." Feel like I'm walking on air.

She barely glances at the envelope. "No we're not millionaires, Mom."

What's *wrong* with her? She's always worrying about money and now that we have it, she seems disinterested.

"It says right here—I won the Sweepstakes. That makes ten—no, twelve million dollars I've won so far. We better claim it before they think we don't want it."

Melissa just stands there, shaking her head like one of those bobble-head dashboard dolls. "This is a gimmick, Mom."

"It can't be. They send me lots of letters. I'll show you." Lead the way to the spare bedroom, fling open the door and point to a huge sack overflowing with envelopes. "Look at this!"

"M-o-m!" Melissa drags out the syllable like a complaint. Everything goes south when she notices my treasure trove piled high on the bed. "Where did all this stuff come from?"

"Dunno."

She runs her long, scarlet fingernails under a tape and opens a box. "This looks like some kind of food processor."

"Dunno."

She checks an invoice. "You must know, Mom. You ordered it."

"If you say so."

Melissa opens one box after another. She finds a foot massager, a chinning bar and a travel iron. We also unpack a cosmetic case filled with twenty different shades of eyeshadow.

I'm thrilled. "This is just like Christmas!"

Melissa sounds annoyed. "Mom, you know you're on a fixed income. What possessed you to buy all these things?"

She's making me look ridiculous. "I bought these diet pills for you and your sister so you can lose some weight." Now Melissa looks offended. Better backtrack. "Actually they're just for Dawn."

"So this is how you maxed out all your credit cards!"

"Who cares? We've got millions of dollars now." Throw a pile of Sweepstakes envelopes in the air and dance a cha-cha step. "This money is for you and your sister. You're going to need it so you can bribe a decent man to marry you. Face it, Melissa, you inherited your father's good looks but money greases the wheels."

Guess that cha-cha was a step too far. Melissa looks kicked to the curb. She sits on the edge of the bed and stares at the floor. When she talks, her voice is taut as a tightrope. "You wasted a lot of money, Mom."

Wasted? "This is for you and Dawn—"

"Don't worry about Dawn. She made some good investments."

Gulp! "Does that mean she's coming to visit?" I'll have to tidy up this bedroom. Surveying the stack of boxes, my stomach twists into a can of worms.

Melissa doesn't seem to notice. "Now that Dawn took early retirement, she has no excuses. It's about time she helped out."

"Doing what?" Talk faster before Melissa wedges in another two cents' worth. "Now I'll have to clean the house and put up all my knick knacks so she can't break them."

Melissa's face goes blank. "Why would she do that?"

"She's such an active little girl, always into everything. You wouldn't think a chubby child could move that fast. Of course it's just baby fat—"

"Dawn's sixty-three, Mom."

What's that supposed to mean? Reminds me of Lewis Carroll, *Alice in Wonderland*. "Half of what she says means something else and the other half doesn't mean anything at all."

Melissa grouses, "I've been after Dawn for months to get her sorry butt out here so we can see a lawyer."

"Papa says you can't trust lawyers."

She won't let it drop. "We have to set up a power of attorney for you and update your will, Mom. In case anything happens."

"Why? What's going to happen?"

Melissa twirls a ring on her finger. Her old habit is a dead-give away that she's lying and trying to cover something up. "One of us may need to take over paying your bills, or make decisions for you."

"The bank pays most of my bills and you cut up my credit cards."

"Look, the truth of the matter is, you probably can't afford to live alone in this house much longer."

"This is about assisted living, isn't it?" I'm in no mood for an argument. Besides, it's almost time for my soap opera. Melissa needs to leave me in peace to enjoy my story.

She keeps prattling. "Yesterday you told Dawn you weren't feeling well when she called. Is something the matter?"

"Yes, it's one o'clock." Head for the living room.

Melissa tags after me. "This is serious, Mom. Tell me if you have any new health issues."

Shrug. "I tell people I'm not feeling well so they'll leave me alone."

Finally! Melissa gets the hint and walks to the door. "I'll call you tonight."

"You do that."

Alone at last! Nestle into my easy chair. Darn that Harry! He left a cup of coffee on the side table without a coaster. "Harry!"

Ah ha, there's lipstick on the cup. So he *is* having an affair...

Oh, that's my shade of lipstick. Must have poured a cup for myself before Melissa started badgering me about credit cards. No point in letting good coffee go to waste but can't take time to reheat it, not when my program is about to start.

What a time for the phone to ring! Take off the receiver to shut it up. A woman's voice keeps saying, "Mom, are you there?"

No, not here. Take a sip of coffee.

My mouth goes numb. Coffee dribbles down the front of my favorite dress.

"Clumsy!" Dab at the stain.

"What?" the voice on the phone asks.

My words slur. "Shom . . . thin's wrong!" The cup slips out of my hand, splattering coffee on the carpet.

Better mop that up before it stains only—can't move!

"Mom? Are you okay?" Dawn's voice drifts over the phone. She sounds faint and faraway, like she's calling from the bottom of a well.

"N—no—" The floor hurtles up, slapping my face. "Help . . . me."

# Chapter 12 TIME OUT

I'm lying in a white bed in a white room with white curtains. Must have died and gone to heaven. Or is this an asylum? Choke down my anxiety and yell, "Where the hell am I?"

Open my eyes, close them. Open them again. A woman in a black dress with vertical white stripes moves toward me like a huge, mutant magpie.

"You're in the hospital, Mom. You had a stroke, but you're going to be alright." She looks vaguely familiar. In fact, she has a curious resemblance to—

Holy Moley, my eighth grade teacher Sister Celestine! Haven't seen that old nun since I was thirteen. She scares the bejeezus out of me!

Hovering over me like a giant penguin she says, "You dodged a bullet."

"Somebody got shot?" Words slosh around in my mouth. Terror splashes down my face, drenching me in sweat.

Sister Celestine glowers at me. "If Dawn hadn't called while you were having a stroke . . . if she hadn't texted me to get help . . ." Her lips flat-line. "You are *so* lucky, Mom. A few more minutes and you could have been paralyzed for life."

Why is this nun calling me "Mom?"

Close my eyes to shut her out but she keeps ranting. "This is a wake-up call. You simply cannot live by yourself anymore."

Pop my eyes open. "Fine. Melissa can sign me up for that dating service." Might not be so bad, shacking up with someone. That would show Harry. What's good for the goose is good for the gander.

Close eyes, open them. Sister Celestine is gone. My daughter Melissa stands by my bed, wearing horizontal pin-stripes that do nothing to compliment her figure. "Mom, did you understand anything I said?"

"That dress does nothing for you."

Melissa drops her eyes. "We can't go on like this."

"Where are we going?"

She sucks in her breath and holds it for so long, she almost turns blue. "Dawn is coming in a couple of days. I've made an appointment to see a lawyer."

"Why? We dodged a bullet, you said so yourself."

Melissa won't make eye contact. "It's time to make some hard decisions, Mom. This is for your own good."

Yeah, right. Mama used to say that when she ladled cod liver oil down my throat.

"Need my beauty rest." Snap my eyes shut so she'll leave me alone.

I conjure up the image of the hallway lined with doors. Opening the right door, I find my way home. Sissy is playing hopscotch on the flagstone walk. Papa is pruning the peach tree and Mama is planting Johnny jump ups in the garden.

"Mom?" Melissa calls me back. Don't want to return. The crimson roses twined onto the trellis in Mama's garden are in full bloom. It's so beautiful here.

"M-o-m! You've got to listen to me." Her voice spreads a greasy smear over the robins-egg-blue sky. Clouds break open; a light rain sprinkles the garden. Colors melt into puddles. The sun shines through the droplets.

When it rains while the sun is shining Mama says, "That means the devil is beating his wife."

Open my eyes, close them. Open my eyes and blink at Melissa.

"Drink . . . water?" My mouth is so dry that my tongue tastes like cotton.

Melissa holds a glass with a straw up to my mouth. The water is deliciously cold like the drinking fountain at City Park. During our last day of school my eighth grade class goes there on a field trip. Sister Celestine scolds me for stepping out of line and sneaking over to the fountain.

Open my eyes, close them. The white walls in the room wrinkle and I'm back in a classroom. Sister Celestine raps her ruler on the blackboard, demanding that we diagram a sentence. Her ruler beats a staccato into my brain.

Words spit out. "Stop it!"

"Sorry," Melissa says as she takes the straw away.

"Need to sleep." Wander down the hallway, opening door after door. They all lead to my eighth grade classroom. Sister Celestine is waiting for me, brandishing her ruler like a sword.

Run away and dash down the hallway opening doors but can't find the one that opens onto Mama's garden.

# **Chapter 13 LOST IN TIME**

Sleep stalks me like a panther lurking in the shadows, watching me with glinting eyes, creeping stealthily on padded feet. Can't let my fears get the better of me, got to stare it down. It growls, slinks into darkness. All the while its eyes glow like fiery coals.

My legs get tangled in a sheet. Fall off the bed, crawl to the door, fling it open. Up ahead, there's a light in the hallway—a nurse's station. Darkness swamps the window above the desk. Is it always night here? Will the sun come up tomorrow?

A nurse looks up with questioning eyes.

Ask her, "Can you roll back the night?"

She doesn't understand and leads me to a door . . . Mama's garden?

No such luck. I'm back in the same white-washed room. Nurse helps me into bed and tucks me in. Slide down a rabbit hole of dreams. This time a door opens onto an ice glazed street. A car rushes past, slams into a telephone pole—

Saints alive! It's Melissa's car! Shattering glass slashes my scream.

I'm still shrieking when a nurse bursts into my room.

"Mrs. Laska, are you all right?" Her kindly eyes calm me. "Would you like a nice, warm blanket?" She brings me one and spreads it over my bed.

"I'm afraid."

"There's nothing to worry about. If you're having trouble sleeping, I'll check with your doctor and see if you can take something."

She's so thoughtful, it would be rude not to gulp down the pill she gives me when she returns.

Everything goes dark.

When the next door opens, bright, coppery light streams through my window. The sun comes up like always!

Words fail me. "Dawn . . . it's dawn . . ."

"Yes, I'm right here, Mom." A plump, middle-aged woman dressed in flaming orange, not angelic white like nurses wear, saunters across the room.

"The sun came up!"

Plump Woman seems amused. "Of course, why wouldn't it?"

"That dress isn't age appropriate." She shakes her head, then smiles like a coquette when a nice-looking young man brings me a tray with my favorite breakfast.

She calls me "Mom" again. What a bold faced lie!

"My daughter was killed in a car accident."

Plump woman wrings her hands and tells the young man, "She's been so irrational lately. Maybe it's her medications." She talks about me like I'm a piece of furniture.

"I'm right here. I can hear you." The words garble with the bite of toast in my mouth. No one seems to care that my precious baby girl is lying dead in some morgue. Tears spill down my cheeks and into my oatmeal.

"It's all right, Mom." Plump woman places a hand on my shoulder.

"Who *are* you?"

She looks hurt. "I'm your oldest daughter, Dawn. I just got in from California. Melissa's at work. Do you want to talk to her?" She picks up the phone and calls. "Hey, can you speak to Mom for a minute? She thinks you were killed in a car accident."

A woman at the other end of the phone line sounds like a spinster school teacher. She's clearly not my little girl in pigtails.

Plump woman pats my arm. "Everything's going to be alright, Mom, you'll see." The agitated tone of her voice tells me everything's not alright and not likely to be alright any time soon.

Don't know what this strange woman expects of me. Better just choke down this breakfast before it goes bad.

# Chapter 14 TOO SOON, NO LONGER JUNE

POP . . . poppity pop pop POP! Firecrackers break open like fluorescent eggshells that shatter outside my window. Bolt upright in bed, tear free of images whirling past me like a swarm of fireflies.

Somewhere outside in the darkness a woman yells, "Knock it off! Fourth of July's over! " Noises keep popping like hammers striking nails.

The people who live on this street must be either rich or stupid because fireworks are expensive. Papa says we don't have money to burn, so we have to choose between fireworks and a watermelon on the Fourth of July. Sissy prefers watermelon, but this year Papa surprises us with sparklers, too. For a whole hour after dark we pretend we're fairies waving magic wands.

Snuggle into my pillow, crawl back into my dream. Papa's taking Sissy and me to a carnival ripe with buttered popcorn and frying onions . . . cotton candy melting in my mouth . . . children on the Ferris wheel squealing as electric lights spark the coal-black sky.

Sissy adores animals and dawdles by the Shetland pony rides. Mama's fascinated by the House of Mirrors. Papa wants to see the wolf boy and the bearded lady at the sideshow.

We wander past booths decorated with red white and blue bunting as a man calls, "Step right up, win a Cupie doll for your little girl!"

Papa stops to pitch balls at a stack of milk cans. He knocks two down and has one to go when Sissy distracts him by tugging at his sleeve.

"Darn you!" Pull her pigtails. Mama tells me to be nice to my sister.

Wake up floundering in darkness. Fall asleep again but can't find my dream. "I'll be a good girl, cross my heart." No one answers me.

The next morning the plump woman who calls herself Dawn asks, "Do you need anything, Mom?"

"Take me to the carnival."

"Sorry, Mom. There's no carnival in town right now." She fusses with my pillow. "Even if there was one, you have to finish rehab before you can go home."

"Is rehab like rewind?"

She rolls her eyes. "This is serious. If you don't do your exercises, you could wind up in a wheelchair."

Heavens to Betsy! Can't let the neighbors see me in a wheelchair! What will they think of me?

When Dawn leans forward, her camellia perfume tickles my nose. "You want to go home, don't you, Mom?"

What kind of question is that?

"The insurance will only pay for another week in this rehab facility. You have to work harder to build up your strength."

"Knucklehead people keep telling me to do stupid things."

"Mom, those exercises will help get you back on your feet."

"What's wrong with my feet?"

Smiling, she pats my hand. "Guess what? I've decided to move back to town and live with you. That way you can stay in your own home."

Want more than anything to go home and find Mama standing at the stove, cooking oatmeal for breakfast—Papa reading his newspaper—Sissy brushing our cat Snowball. "Is my cat OK?"

The woman who calls herself Dawn raises a pencil-thin eyebrow. "You don't have a cat. But if you really want one, maybe we can adopt one from the Pound."

"Why would we do that?" Snowball is the most beautiful cat in the world. He's silky white with sky-blue eyes. Knot my fists and chant, "Want Snowball! Want Snowball!"

A woman who has cleavage and cherry red hair enters my room carrying a clipboard. "We all want snowballs, Honey. This July heatwave is for the birds."

She looks familiar—too familiar. After she leaves, whisper to Dawn, "Was that Bernice?"

Dawn's two penciled eyebrows crinkle into one. "Who's Bernice?"

"The dirty no-count bitch who ran off with your father."

"Mom!"

"That dirty no-count bitch Bernice is having an affair with him. Your sister helped drive them to Las Vegas."

"Now Mom—" Dawn acts like she doesn't believe me. She grabs my hand. Pull it away.

"Help me find my purse before that no-count bitch Bernice steals it."

Dawn talks slow, real slow. "Listen, Mom. Daddy never had an affair. The only Bernice I know cleaned the house for us thirty years ago when you broke your ankle."

"Yep, that's the right Bernice! The dirty low-down bitch."

"Bernice is probably dead by now."

"Oh no, she's too smart for that." Now where's my purse? "It was right here on the dresser—"

"Is this it?" Dawn looks behind a chair and holds up my brown suede bag.

"You see? That dirty no-count bitch Bernice probably put it there." Open big handbag, take out small, pretty purse with sequins.

Plump Woman rolls eyes. "Mom, why are you carrying two purses?"

Stupid question. "Little purse is for the things I need. Big purse is for everything else."

Dawn looks incredibly tired for someone who was named for the break of day. "A soon as you finish your rehab, Mom, you can go home and you won't have to worry about Bernice anymore."

Home. The word is as tantalizing as the sugary fragrance of Mama's chocolate chip cookies. "Let's go now."

Dawn takes a sudden interest in a picture of sunflowers hanging on the wall. "I've been thinking, your house is way too big for just the two of us. I'm looking into condos."

"Condoms?"

"Condos." Dawn raises her voice like I'm deaf. "That way we won't have a yard to keep up."

Sounds like she's trying to weasel out of work, just like the times she doesn't want to take her turn drying dishes.

She tries to butter me up by saying, "This is my chance to pay you back for being such a good mother."

"My Mama went to every PTA meeting and made treats for my school's Halloween party."

Dawn gets quiet. She finally says, "Mom, we've had our differences from time to time—"

"What time is it?"

She takes a deep breath. "I want to make a fresh start. You and Melissa have a great relationship and I'd like us to have one, too."

She's looking me straight in the eye. Is this a staring contest?

OK, just stare back, try not to blink.

"Do you think we can do that, Mom?"

Whoever blinks first, loses.

She pats my hand.

I blink. Darn, don't win anything.

Dawn keeps pestering me about how she wants a relationship, whatever that is. It's like she's a five-year-old kid begging for the life-size doll that they keep advertising on television.

Dawn squeezes my hand until it hurts. "I'm so grateful I could take an early retirement, Mom. I just hope it's not too late for us."

"It's never too late." That's what Papa says. Yank my hand away. Thank heavens she goes to the window and mumbles to herself.

Now to hide my purse before that damn Bernice steals it. This Dawn-Woman is probably in cahoots with her. Stash my purse under a pillow and chuckle to myself. Just let that dirty bitch Bernice find it now!

# Chapter 15 ONCE UPON ANOTHER TIME

Home sweet home! Never want to leave again. So why is the woman who calls herself Dawn dragging me out to a restaurant to eat? We have a refrigerator full of food.

Dawn keeps flipping from Miss Sugar and Spice to Sister Celestine. Why is she driving me in the car if she doesn't like me? "Just take me home."

She rolls her eyes. "Mom, please stop saying that. And leave your seat belt on."

Her car is making high, squeaky noises like a love crazed cricket. Snap the buckle back into the little box tucked next to my seat. The noise stops like magic.

"Let's go home."

"Now Mom, Melissa and I went to a lot of trouble to arrange this. We think it's important to celebrate milestone birthdays and happy occasions."

She's such a martyr. "It's not my birthday."

"Yes, it is. Melissa insisted we have a party—"

Always up to no good. "Do whatever you want, just leave me out of it."

Dawn sweetens her voice like Mama does when she's trying to trick me into eating spinach. "You don't want to miss your own birthday party, do you?"

"Yep, sure do."

She belches out a sigh as we pull into a parking lot overflowing with cars next to a long, low building with glittery windows.

Oh goody, there are no parking spaces. "We might as well leave."

Dawn parks in a handicap spot.

"You can't park here. We'll get a ticket."

"No, I've got this." She hangs a blue and white card on the rear view mirror, then opens the trunk to get a wheelchair out. Pretty darn clever. It'll fool people into thinking she's handicapped.

She tries to get me into the wheelchair but I'm not playing her game.

Dawn is a little less sweet now. "Honestly, Mom, do you think you can walk to the door by yourself?"

"No, so take me home."

Dawn nudges the wheelchair closer. "Melissa and I went to a lot of expense to throw you this party."

Why did my daughter Melissa drag this Dawn woman into my personal business?

"Yo!" A young man with wildly curling hair ambles up to us.

In the blink of an eye Dawn turns into a charmer. "Mom, this is your sister's grandson Ted. His family came all the way from Tucson for your big day. Isn't that great?"

"That's a lot of trouble." Squint at him. "He doesn't look like Sissy."

Ted grins. "Want me to push your wheelchair, Aunt Rhea?"

"Sure, why not?" He sure is handsome, wonder if he has a girlfriend? Put my hand on his shoulder as he helps me out of the car and into the wheelchair. I'm expecting a ride around the parking lot, but instead he pushes me right through the front door into a noisy restaurant jam packed with people, all squished together like sardines.

They all act like they know me. Just smile, play along by saying nonsense like, "It's so nice to see you." Even though it isn't.

Dawn has a silly, plastic grin on her face when Melissa strolls up, hanging onto a tall man in a cowboy hat.

Melissa seems proud of herself. "Mom, I want you to meet Wayne."

"Are you going to marry her?" He turns red. That makes me think he's already married and is cheating on his wife.

Choking on a laugh Melissa says, "Mom's quite the joker."

They think *I'm* a joke? "Are you a real cowboy or did you just buy the hat?"

By now Wayne is so red, he looks like he's suffering from sun stroke but he says, "Fact is, I do own a ranch and raise Angus."

While Melissa and Dawn whisper together, he explains that Angus are a type of cow. That's the most useful information I've heard all day and I'm starting to like him. When Melissa comes back, I take Wayne's hand and tell her, "You were gone too long. He's mine now." Melissa laughs again like she really thinks I'm joking.

She pushes my wheelchair to a table piled with gifts. "Look, Mom, you have presents." She probably wants me to forget about Wayne.

Must be Christmas! Love opening gifts. Sissy and I scour the house to find where Mama and Papa hid our presents. She knows how to slip off the ribbon then roll a pencil under the tape to loosen it so we can slide the wrapping off. We re-wrap the packages and pretend we're surprised on Christmas morning.

Don't see Sissy anywhere so tear the pretty wrapping paper real careful. Inside a box is a plush white cat that looks a lot like my Snowball. "You're back!" His fur is satin-soft rubbing against my face. But this Snowball doesn't purr. He doesn't even squirm.

Dawn helps me open the other presents—mostly clothes. Nothing that I want.

Melissa rolls me up to a table and brings me a plate from the buffet.

Take a big bite and say, "This is so much better than what we get at home." Uh-oh, shouldn't have said that. Wayne might not marry Melissa if he thinks she can't cook.

Melissa looks flustered. "Time for your cake, Mom." She pushes my wheelchair toward a huge cake loaded down with candles.

"Make a wish and blow them out."

Don't have enough breath and Snowball is useless. "Just get the fire extinguisher." Everyone laughs. Melissa must have told them I'm a joke.

While I eat cake, Melissa taps her spoon on a water glass. It has a nice ring to it—piano lessons finally paid off.

She says, "My sister Dawn put together a powerpoint highlighting Mom's life."

Who's Dawn?

After someone piddles with a contraption, a parade of pictures dance across a screen.

Something's not right! Real people don't look fuzzy like that. These pictures look like the fun mirrors at a carnival that make you look too fat or too tall.

My blood runs cold. Tug at Melissa's sleeve. "Have to go!"

Melissa flinches. "Just a few more minutes, Mom."

"Have to go now!" Point to a door at random.

"You need to use the restroom? Why didn't you say so?" She pushes my wheelchair away from the table.

Now we're getting somewhere! Except people keep stopping us and talking about somebody's birthday.

Make it to the bathroom just in time. On the way back Melissa gushes, "Isn't this nice, Mom? Your whole family's here."

Don't see Mama or Papa or Sissy. My family's not here except for Snowball. Hug him, peer up at Melissa. "We better go home. Mama is waiting up for me."

Melissa's smile freezes. "No, she isn't."

How does she know? Gawk around. Some people kind of look familiar. Get up my guts and ask one of them for a ride home.

Melissa apologizes. Her smile slips off her face like a sunny-side-up egg sliding off a plate.

Hold everything—Sissy's at the next table! "You're here! You came to see me!"

She reaches out and clasps my hand. "I wouldn't miss this for anything, Aunt Rhea."

Melissa says, "This is Sissy's granddaughter Allison."

"Granddaughter?" Close my eyes, open them. "You do look just like Sissy. You're so pretty."

"Thank you, Aunt Rhea."

"Are you an artist like Sissy?

"Why yes, I am."

"Sissy did the most elaborate charcoal drawings of horses. Is that what you do?"

"No, I do commercial art. I'm not as talented as she was."

"Give yourself time, you're still young. I'm so happy you're here." Smiles butter both our faces.

When we come back to Plump Woman's table she asks, "Are you enjoying your party, Mom?"

Why does she keep calling me "Mom?"

Melissa pushes my wheelchair closer to Plump Woman and says, "I'm handing her off to you. Good luck." She sits next to a cowboy across the table.

Settle Snowball on my lap so he can look up at me with his bright blue eyes. "Ready to go home now. I'm tired of talking."

Plump woman's smile flips upside down. "OK, Mom. I'll take you home."

# Chapter 16 BY AND BY

Plump Woman leaves the house to go to a place called The Pound.

"Bon Voyage!" I yell as she closes the door. Now to eat cookies in bed.

She comes back way too soon lugging a large box into the house. "Look at this, Mom." Why does she call me that?

When Plump Woman opens the box, a black cat peeks out.

"I love cats!" Stroke his head. He rubs against me and purrs. This new cat doesn't look like the white cat from my birthday party. He's got shifty eyes and a twitchy tail.

Tell Plump Woman, "Think I'll call him Black Snowball." This is the nicest thing she's done for me since she's been here. Pet his silky head and say, "Thank you."

"I'm so glad you like the cat, Mom. You love your toy cat so much, I thought you would like a real one to keep you company."

Black Snowball sniffs at White Snowball who doesn't sniff back. Some things don't add up. Makes me feel like I'm losing it.

In no time at all Black Snowball is my favorite cat. He runs and jumps like a monkey. But he stops and purrs when I run my hand down his long, slinky back. He's also perfectly happy to sit on my lap when he's not eating or pawing around in his litter box or scratching furniture.

White Snowball doesn't do much of anything. He just sits and stares, even when he sleeps. It's nice to live alone with my two cats, but Plump Woman won't leave. She has the gall to move into the room down the hall. Maybe she's here to keep the house clean. Mama wouldn't approve of all the dust bunnies under the couch. Sister Celestine would slap my wrist and ask me why I need somebody to help me dust.

Plump Woman comes into the living room where I'm watching the clouds outside the window with Black Snowball on my lap. We try to decide if they look like the sheep we're supposed to count when we fall asleep.

"Here's a present for you, Mom."

Plump Woman's teeth are yellow with coffee stains but that doesn't keep her from smiling as she hands me a box.

Shake the box—it jingles! "Goody, a set of jacks!" Sissy can scoop up eight jacks at a time. Not me, can only grab five.

"Why don't you open it, Mom?"

Black Snowball is purring, letting me know he wants to see what's in the box, too. Hold up a handful of dangly silver tubes that clink when they knock together. We're both disappointed.

"What's this supposed to be?"

Plump Woman is still smiling. "It's a wind chime. We used to have one like this on the porch years ago."

What porch is she talking about?

When the tubes jangle together it sounds like they're saying, "Clickety clack, clickety clack, your husband's gone and he won't be back." Put them back in the box so they shut up.

Plump Woman keeps talking, "I've been thinking of fun things we can do together, Mom. You always loved the theater. When was the last time you went?"

"Dunno."

Plump Woman's smile gets wider and yellower. She holds up two scraps of red paper. "I have two tickets for the repertory theater. They're performing a show that won a Tony award."

"Dunno."

That usually stops a conversation in its tracks. Not this time.

IT'S SCARY SITTING here in the dark theater with all the lights turned off except for a big floodlight up at the front of this humongous room. A handful of people are standing in the light, babbling nonsense.

Turn to Plump Woman sitting beside me and say, "Isn't this the most boring thing you ever saw? I want to go home."

A mean woman in front of us turns around and puts her finger to her lips.

"Shush!"

Tell her, "Well it is."

Plump Woman's sigh feels warm in my ear. "When the lights come back up, we'll go home."

"Good. Mama is waiting up for me."

On the drive home Plump Woman says, "Guess I need to realize that you no longer enjoy going to events."

"That's not true. There are plenty of places I enjoy."

"Tell me where you'd like to go, Mom."

Think a minute. "Take me to City Park. Papa always takes me there. Sometimes he lets me ride on the carousel. It only costs a nickel."

Plump Woman laughs. "Those days are long gone."

"Where did they go?"

"I'll take you to the park when the weather's good. Would you also like to go to the zoo?"

"Yes! Love seeing monkeys."

"When you took Melissa and me to the zoo, we enjoyed the monkey house, too. Afterwards you always bought us an ice cream cone."

Look at her. Close my eyes, open them. "You like strawberry. Melissa likes chocolate."

"Yes, Mom, glad you remember. Those were the good old days."

Feels good to laugh together. This seems like the right time to tell her that she's going the wrong way.

"No, I'm not."

"This isn't our street."

Her voice is crisp as bacon. "Yes, it is."

"We live on Fourth Avenue."

"No Mom, you lived there when you were a little girl."

What's she talking about? "Just take me home!" Instead she parks in a strange driveway.

"We're home, Mom." She leads the way inside a yellow stucco house that looks a little familiar. Think I've been here before.

We go inside. Where's Mama's mahogany dining room table? That's her pride and joy. Papa bought it at an auction when a fancy hotel downtown went out of business.

Stomp my foot. "Take me home right now!"

Plump Woman wilts like a bloomed-out rose. She gestures to the pictures on the living room wall. "Now Mom, why would anyone else have pictures of *our* family on *their* wall?"

Guess that makes sense.

She leads me down the hallway. "Here's your bedroom."

Isn't my room upstairs? Sunlight wakes me each morning when it flows through the east window and plays tricks with the ivy wallpaper, making it look like it's alive.

There's no sun to play tricks on me now; night fills the window.

Sit on the edge of a much-too-large bed. It's frightening, being locked up in this strange room. Then Black Snowball pounces on my lap just like a monkey.

"Thank heavens you're here." I stroke his sleek, silky fur as he purrs. Everyone else abandoned me.

Tiptoe to the door and peek down the hall. Plump Woman is getting into Harry's hooch, pouring herself a stiff one. Wish she'd pour me a drink, too.

# Chapter 17 ENDLESS SUMMER

Black Snowball flicks his tail and plays with a long string of perfectly good dental floss hanging out of a wastebasket. "We can reuse this." Roll it into a neat ball. "Waste not, want not, that's what Mama always says." She saves grease, tin cans, rubber bands, Clorox bottles, cardboard boxes, newspapers—

Black Snowball curls his tail into a question mark and follows me to Plump Woman's room to put the ball of string on her vanity table.

Left another ball here . . . pretty sure we did . . . is this the right room? They all seem to mush together.

Now where to put this for safekeeping? Maybe in the jewelry box?

Plump Woman's voice sounds sharp and loud. "Dinner's ready!" Black Snowball dashes into the hallway. Only speaks cat but he knows the word "dinner."

Reach the kitchen. Tall woman with hair knotted in a bun at the back of her neck is standing by the stove. My heart thumps faster. "Mama, is that you?"

She turns to me. Disappointed. "You're not my Mama."

"No, I'm your daughter Dawn. Why don't you sit down, I have dinner ready."

"Thanks, nice to be waited on."

Black Snowball pounces onto a chair. Papa wouldn't like that but he's not here.

"No kitties at the table." Plump Woman tries to shoo him away.

Push back my plate. "Won't eat if Snowball can't eat." Yuck. She's giving me mystery meat, peas and potatoes. "Phooey on this food."

Plump Woman looks tired, like she's been slaving over a hot stove all day. "Cats don't eat people's food. You know that, Mom." But Snowball acts like he's willing to try it. Jumps back on chair and sniffs my plate.

"Mom!" Plump Woman's upset because Snowball won't eat her mystery meat.

What to do? Everything tastes better with sugar. Should be in the cupboard.

"Mom, what are you looking for?" Plump Woman frowns at me rummaging through shelves.

Can't find the word. "Uh . . . uh . . . sugar." Fumble around. Cans fall out and bang on the countertop, nearly hit me on the head.

Slink back to chair. "Sorry, should have minded you." Bet Mama and Papa hired Plump Woman to babysit me while they went dancing. Now I'm in trouble!

Plump Woman mumbles as she puts the cans away. Good time to hide my peas in this napkin. Mama gives me a cookie for eating vegetables but I hate peas.

Hold up plate when Plump Woman comes back to the table. "Finished! How about a cookie please?"

"Why don't you have a tangerine?" Plump Woman takes one out of a bowl and starts to peel it.

Hmmm . . . Smells like Christmas. "Santa always puts an orange in our stockings."

Lean over the table to take a better whiff. Napkin slides off my lap. Peas scatter all over the floor. Snowball helps hide them by batting them under the stove.

Plump Woman frowns. Have to convince her I'm a good girl or I'll never get a cookie. Better finish that crossword puzzle before she nags me. Only, can't make the letters fit in those tiny little boxes.

Got to find another game. "Let's play find-the-button."

"That old game?" Plump Woman's laugh jiggles her frown away. "Oh Mom, we haven't played that game since Melissa and I were in grade school." Her mouth curls into a smile. "We spent hours trying to figure out where you hid that button. It must have kept us kids out of your hair for hours."

"You were a kid?" She's too tall. "You're pulling my leg."

"Of course I was a kid, I was *your* kid." Plump Woman goes to the living room, comes back and shows me a photograph. "Here's Melissa and me dressed up like princesses for Halloween."

"No, that's me and Sissy. She double dared me to knock on the big mansion at the end of our block that we thought was haunted."

Plump Woman asks, "Did you do it?"

"Yep. They gave me a whole lot of candy, too. Sissy was so jealous."

Look over my shoulder. "Haven't seen Sissy lately."

Plump Woman's voice gets quiet. "She passed away, Mom."

Mom, who's Mom?

Plump Woman takes the photograph back and brings me another one. "We took this about five years ago at Melissa's house."

Merciful heavens! Two old biddies sitting on porch swing are holding the ugliest children on earth. My voice cracks. "Are those your kids?"

Plump Woman laughs. "They're Melissa's dogs, Mom. She likes Pekingese."

Squint at photograph. "Oh, thank the Lord."

I blink several times. "Dawn? Is that you?"

She beams. "Yes, Mom. It's me."

"You live in California, don't you?"

"That's right. But I came back to take care of you, Mom."

"That makes me so happy, Dawn. But I should be taking care of you."

"No Mom, it's my turn."

My heart fills with joy. "You're a wonderful daughter."

She reaches over and hugs me tight.

When she lets go, I take the picture and study it. "You would have made a wonderful mother, Dawn."

Tears roll down her cheek and she looks at the floor. "I wanted children, but when I found out that Tony was unfaithful, I divorced him." Her voice breaks. "Some of my friends knew and didn't tell me. It was so humiliating."

Hug her again. "Oh Sweetie."

"You haven't called me that in years."

Don't know what else to say so just hug her tight. She hugs me back.

Look over her shoulder at the dark window. Mama is waiting up for me. Tell Plump Woman, "It's time to go home."

"You mean it's time for you to go to bed. But speaking of home, there's something I need to explain." She folds her hands like she's getting ready to pray. "I'll do my darndest to keep you here in your own house, Mom. We have to make this work for the next five years, otherwise we'll have to sell your house and use the proceeds to pay for a nursing home. Melissa should have transferred your savings and house title to our names years ago to save your assets, but you made such a fuss about it that she let it slide."

Slide . . . slides on a playground . . . slide rule in high school. "Never was good at math."

Plump Woman's face wrinkles up. "Well I've done the math. You don't have enough savings to pay for more than six months of care in a good nursing home. Then you'll have to go on Medicaid."

All this math is making my head ache. "Just take me home."

"You are home, Mom."

Sit there staring at each other.
Plump Woman blinks first and looks away.
Chalk up a win up for my side! Expect a cookie but don't get one.
Life isn't fair.

# Chapter 18 CAT DAYS OF SUMMER

Smiley Lady is in cahoots with Plump Woman. She's nice at first, then says, "Let's take a shower, Miz Rhea." Everything goes to hell in a handbasket.

Shiver with cold when she runs water down my back. Can't help swearing like a drunken sailor. "Damn you, Bitch!" Take a swing at her. She just keeps smiling and whistling, scrubbing my back while water splashes out of the wall, hitting my face like hailstones. Scream at the top of my lungs. "Where the hell are my clothes?"

I'm freezing to death, standing here naked as a jaybird in the rain.

Smiley Lady can afford to smile—she isn't getting slapped with cold water. She talks down to me. "Now Miz Rhea, you know you need to wash up."

"Hate you!"

"You don't like this one bit, I get that. But your daughter says you gotta keep clean."

"Like hell!" Double my fist, shake it in her face. Can't think of right words to say. Want to tell her where to go and how to get there. All that dribbles out of my mouth is,

"Damn, damn, damn, damn, damn."

Why is she doing this to me? My horrible daughter Melissa or that Plump Woman must have put her up to it.

"Want to go home!" Can't Smiley Lady see I'm Pitiful Little Girl who just needs her Mama?

Finally! Water stops and Smiley Lady wraps me in a fluffy towel. This is more like it. She dries my head with steel thing that blows nice, warm wind through my hair.

She puts wind away in cabinet then picks up shiny gold tube. People who live here must be rich if they can afford to leave gold lying around their house.

"Would you like to put on a little lipstick?" Smiley Lady asks and opens the tube. "Everyone looks better with lipstick." She touches my lips, then rubs fog off silvery window over the sink. "Take a look at yourself in the mirror, Miz Rhea."

Old woman squints back at me.

Someone hollers from the end of the hallway. Smiley Lady goes to the door and yells, "Don't you worry, Miz Dawn, I'll stay with her until you get back."

Old Woman in mirror would look better with lipstick . . . hard to draw on steamy glass.

"Don't do that, Miz Rhea!" Smiley Lady takes the tube away. When she wipes the mirror, Old Woman gawks at us. Look over shoulder. Where is she? Smiley Lady and me are only people here. Old Woman must be a ghost.

Smiley Lady takes an old-fashioned dress off a hook on the back of the door. "You like blue, don't you, Miz Rhea?"

"No, Sissy likes blue, not me."

She stops smiling. "Let me get you another dress. You stay right here." When she opens the door to go out, Black Snowball slinks into bathroom and purrs.

Smiley Lady comes back with a green dress. Don't like green either but she's trying to be nice so don't make a fuss.

Tell Smiley Lady, "Mama says you should always look your best. You never know when a nice young gentleman is going to call."

Smiley Lady laughs. "You got that right, Miz Rhea."

So happy to get something right!

"Let's watch some TV," Smiley says.

Black Snowball leads the way out of the hot bathroom to the nice cool living room.

"You sit in your chair, Miz Rhea. Here's your toy cat." Smiley turns on infernal noise box. Pictures jump around like crazed rabbits. All that gibberish makes my head ache but Mama says little girls should do their darndest to be polite.

Black Snowball curls into my lap along with white Snowball. Smiley Lady sits in Harry's chair.

"You can't sit there! My husband will be back soon."

"I'll move just as soon as he comes in." But Smiley Lady falls asleep and starts to snore. Harry will have a fit when he comes back from tinkering in the garage and finds her sleeping in his chair.

Got to get out of here. Don't want to hear him cuss. White Snowball falls on the floor. Black Snowball hops over him.

Want to get out of ugly green dress. Black Snowball leads me to sunny room at end of hallway with four poster bed and vanity table frilled in pink ruffles.

Ask Black Snowball, "What did we come here for?" He purrs. That's right, different dress.

"Mama says to put on clean underwear first." The dresser drawer is full of lacey undies. Black Snowball hops up and sniffs. He looks disappointed that there's nothing to eat.

Doesn't look like there's anything to wear, either. "These look awfully skimpy." Hold up underwear. Probably won't fit over my wide hips.

Black Snowball twitches his tail toward vanity table. Little gold scissors glint in sunlight. They're so tiny, takes forever to snip elastic from bras and panties. "There. They should fit just fine now." Black Snowball purrs.

"Now we need gloves and matching purse." He helps me search the closet. "Damn that low-down bitch Bernice, she ran off with my husband and took all my clothes."

Shuffle back to the living room. Noise box still blaring. Man in the box says, "Don't touch that dial—"

Fine. Pound on it to shut it off.

That wakes up Smiley Lady. "Use the changer, Miz Rhea, don't hit the TV." She hands me a plastic gizmo. "Here, find a program you like."

Click, click, click. Pictures jump in and out of the screen. Clickety, click. Pleasant Looking Man sells shiny rings for low-low price of $19.95.

Tell Smiley Lady. "Write a check so it won't cost anything."

She laughs. "Now Miz Rhea, what do you want with some cheap ring? You got a real diamond on your finger." She snatches plastic gizmo back. "Let's find something else to watch."

Still looking when Melissa and Plump Woman come in carrying shopping bags.

"We got you some new house shoes, Mom," Melissa says. "Your old ones were getting ratty."

Plump Woman says. "You needed a new nightgown, too."

Melissa smiles at me. "We stopped by the Candy Corner for your favorite fudge. They also opened a bakery." She opens a box of cupcakes topped with cherries.

Tell them, "My baby girls love cupcakes, too."

"Yes we do, Mom." Plump Woman's grin splits her face. "We had tea parties in the backyard all the time when we were kids."

Look around. "Need hats and gloves."

Smiley Lady steps out of shadows. "There's some hat boxes in the hall closet. I'll go get them for you."

"Would you like a cupcake, Edna?" Melissa asks.

"Thank you but I best be getting home." Smiley Lady brings hat boxes then leaves.

Melissa and Plump Woman laugh as they put on silly hats so large they flop down, almost hide their faces. Find my special occasion hat with pink roses. Put it on, reach for cupcakes.

"These are almost as good as the ones you make," Melissa says.

Me? Make cupcakes?

Shrug. They think I'm someone else.

# Chapter 19 SOME SOME SUMMERTIME

Close my eyes, imagine walking down long hallway, looking for door to Mama's garden. Open eyes when Plump Woman yells, "Edna, can you help me with these groceries?"

"Sure enough, Miz Dawn," Smiley Lady gets out of Harry's chair, steps over White Snowball sleeping on floor with eyes open. Black Snowball runs to kitchen, comes back to sit in sun and wash paws.

Plump Woman walks by, pets his head. "Such a nice kitty."

"No one pet me today."

"Okay, Mom." Plump Woman comes over, gives me hug.

She goes down hallway, shrieks, comes back holding black lace bra. "What happened to this?"

"Dunno."

She's red like pickled beets. "This cost eighty dollars, Mom! I have to buy specialty bras because of my cup size." She goes to the kitchen, talks to Smiley Lady.

Ask Black Snowball, "Is something wrong with me?"

Smiley Lady comes in. "I'll be staying a little longer, Miz Rhea. Would you like to play cards?" She takes a deck out of her pocket.

"Goody! Can we play Fish?" That's my favorite. We call out the little red or black numbers and whoever wins the most cards gets a cookie. That's always me.

Smiley Lady holds her cards like a fan. Should do that too, but need to keep my eye on Plump Woman. She's in the hallway, digging Harry's liquor stash out of a closet. Didn't think anyone else knew where he hides his hooch.

Lord Almighty, she's drinking right out of the bottle! Better add water to it so Harry won't know she's guzzling his booze.

If he finds out, I'll lose my housekeeper. Can't let that happen!

# **Chapter 20 SLEEPY TIME**

Open my eyes. I'm in a strange, dark house. Hide under the sheets until . . . Uh-oh, have to go to the bathroom. Something rustling under the bed? Feel around with my big toe. "Monsters, don't grab my leg!" Slide ever so carefully out of bed, thick carpet feels warm and soft. Follow hallway light to bathroom.

Scared because no one's around. What would Sissy do? Dial 911! A pleasant sounding woman answers and asks, "What is your emergency?"

Good question. "My family takes care of me, but they left me all alone in this big spooky house."

Pleasant Woman sounds worried. "Do you require medical assistance?"

Since she's offering, why not? "Yes, oh yes!"

"I'll send help." Pleasant Woman tells me to stay on phone. She's so much nicer than Plump Woman, who grumbled for hours that her underwear is cut to pieces.

Sirens split the quiet night. Red lights sparkle in front of house just like Fourth of July fireworks.

Sharp knock on front door. "Did you call for assistance, ma'am?" Handsome Policeman asks.

"Hello, it's so nice of you to drop by."

Policeman has deep sounding voice. "You told the dispatcher you've been left alone."

"Mom, what's going on?"

For Pete's sake! Plump Woman shuffles to the door looking like a dog's breakfast in that tacky bathrobe of hers. Pink is definitely not her color. Her hair's a mess and it's a good thing she gets her sash tied before she's arrested for indecent exposure. Looking that way won't impress a man.

Handsome Policeman pretends not to notice. "We got a 911 call—"

Plump Woman doesn't let him finish. "There must be some mistake."

"No mistake. This elderly lady said she's home alone and requires medical assistance."

Quit looking at me!

Plump Woman doesn't make sense. "My mother tends to get confused from time to time. I'm her daughter and live here with her. I'm sorry for the misunderstanding, officer."

He is so nice, I'm sorry to see him go. "Such a nice young man. You should give him your phone number."

Plump Woman shuts the door then leans against it. "M-o-m." She drags out the word.

What's her problem? "You want to get married, don't you? Isn't that why you signed up for that dating service?"

"You're mixing me up with Melissa." She runs her hand through her hair, sighs. "You seem to be getting more and more confused. We need to talk to your doctor."

"Is he good looking?"

"It doesn't matter."

"Well, you look like death warmed over. If you expect to meet someone, you need to dress better."

Plump Woman stifles a yawn. "It's three am. Let's go back to bed. We can talk about this in the morning."

Three am *is* morning. "I'm not sleepy. Why don't we call 911 again and talk to someone who's not grumpy."

She shakes her head. "How about a cup of hot chocolate, Mom? That always helps you sleep."

Who's Mom?

Sit at the dining room table and wait while Grumpy Woman goes to the kitchen. She comes back with a cup of hot chocolate. It's perfect, topped with tiny marshmallows.

Grumpy Woman sits down and starts to drum on the table. Her fingernails are painted a pretty shade of red but they're chipped around the edges. She drums and drums and drums.

# **Chapter 21 TWILIGHT TIME**

Cereal box reads, "Instant oatmeal—cooks in five minutes." Stomach is growling but Plump Woman is outside talking loud to someone. Don't see anybody. Guess it's up to me to cook something. Follow directions: set box on stove, turn on burner and count five minutes.

One minute . . . two . . . three . . . four . . . box breaks into flames!

"Stop that!" Fire doesn't listen to me. It gobbles up cereal box.

Black Snowball folds back ears and runs out pet door. Hope he's going for help.

What would Sissy do?

Grab spray nozzle from sink, aim for stove. Water shoots across kitchen. Red-orange flames hiss, crackle and pop. Screeching noise on ceiling hurts my eardrums.

"Take that!" Spray more water. Alarm keeps blaring. More fire on stove.

Water down stove until alarm stops. Tiny flames almost gone. Snatch dish rag, beat them out.

Open back door, set smoke free.

"You can come in now, Black Snowball!" He just sits under the apple tree. Too smart to breathe smoke.

Stare at kitchen. Soot blackens walls, making me cough. Water drips from ceiling, dribbles down my neck. Ashes all over stove, smear into muddy puddle onto the floor.

"Uh-oh. Whoever made this mess is in a lot of trouble."

Must hide evidence. What to do with burned dishtowel?

"Garbage disposal!" Stuff dish towel down hole in sink.

Front door opens. "Mom, I smell smoke!"

"Dunno." Shove dishtowel deep down black hole.

Plump Woman comes into kitchen. Her mouth falls open. "What on earth—?"

"Dunno."

"Can't I leave you alone for five minutes?"

"Dunno."

Plump Woman slaps mop around floor, scrubs stove.

Still hungry but not a good time to ask for cookies. Steal saltine crackers out of box on counter.

Backdoor open. "Snowball want a cracker?" Black Snowball stretches then washes toes. "Be like that!" Bet White Snowball wants a cracker.

He's not hungry but he lets me brush him. White Snowball always sits still even when fur comes out in clumps. Brush Black Snowball too. He sheds fur on everything.

White Snowball watches me eat crackers then sweep crumbs under rug. Tuck him under arm, go to living room to sit by window. Sun bath feels nice and warm, not like chilly water baths Smiley Lady gives me.

Close my eyes, wander down hallway, open door. This isn't Mama's house! Shadowy room crammed with cobwebs. Giant spider lives here spinning nets to catch flies.

Door slams shut behind me. Crowd rushes by, tears through cobwebs. So many people talking—

Open eyes. Someone *is* in kitchen talking.

Sneak up to door. Dead body lying on the floor, its head under sink.

Holy Moley, Plump Woman is standing there. Looks like she killed someone!

Tingle with shivers. Throat too tight to scream!

Man pokes head out from underneath cabinet—he's not dead!

Big, greasy grin on face. He holds up burnt dish towel. "Here's your problem. This was stuck in your garbage disposal."

Plump Woman sees me. "Mom, do you know anything about this?"

"Dunno." Slip hand in pocket; cross fingers to be on safe side.

Plump Woman frowns. That means she won't give me cookie.

Black Snowball comes back inside. We go to living room and dig secret candy stash out from underneath couch. Don't like peppermint, it's Sissy's favorite. Only eat it when there's nothing else.

Plump Woman comes into living room, sits down on couch.

Hold out peppermint candy but she doesn't take it.

"Mom, we've got to make this work."

Make what work?

"The alternative is—you won't be able to stay in your home anymore."

Take candy out of mouth. Don't want it anymore. Sissy teases always, says Mama and Papa will send me away. Can't let that happen.

# **Chapter 22 END TIME**

Go to my room to hide. Devil hops on my shoulder. His voice smells like whiskey. "Harry left a loaded gun in the closet. You *could* shoot yourself. That would solve all your problems."

Angel climbs on other shoulder, shakes finger. "Don't you dare do such a knucklehead thing!"

Devil keeps sweet-talking. "The gun's hidden in a cardboard box under Harry's funeral programs. That's why Melissa and Dawn didn't find it when they cleared out his clothes and gave them to the Salvation Army."

Angel scolds, "Don't you dare do anything foolish!"

Devil makes sense. "You better act fast before they send you away. Then you'll never come home again."

Open closet door. Devil lies a lot but not this time! Gun right here in box where he said it would be.

Gun looks like the one that the Boy Who Lives Down Street shows me and Sissy. He climbs on a chair, gets gun down from shelf. Shows us how to load it. Says he can shoot to kill.

The Boy Who Lives Down Street has a problem with his blood. Goes to sleep, never wakes up.

Tell Angel, "Want to go to sleep like that."

Her halo wobbles. "It's not your decision."

Devil laughs. "Sure it is. It's your right to decide when and how you want to leave this world." Breath smells like sour milk. "Plump Woman's outside on the porch right now, talking on her cell phone. This is the one chance you've got to check out of here before she sends you away forever. Better grab it while you can."

Angel shakes head. "Don't do it. If you shoot yourself, you'll make her mad."

Devil laughs louder. "What do you care? You'll be dead."

Run my hand over Harry's gun. Feels smooth, heavy, cold.

Devil looks at door. "Hurry, or it'll be too late."

Angel sits on gun. "Put it down this minute!"

Devil claps claws. "Do it, do it!"

Lift gun as Devil grins. "It's loaded. All you have to do is pull the trigger."

Angel frowns. "Papa says not to play with guns."

Devil limps on crooked feet. "You want to see your Papa again, don't you? He and Mama and Sissy are waiting for you."

Hands shake bad. Pull trigger.

Shot clangs like marbles Sissy drops down grate. They clatter all the way to furnace in basement. Mama is so mad!

Knock Devil over, dump gun in box, shove in closet, slam door.

Holy Smoke! Hole in door stares back at me.

Devil shrugs. "Tell Plump Woman it was an accident."

Angel punches him. "No, tell her the truth."

Better idea. Grab post card off dresser. Bet it's from Harry on his honeymoon with that damn dirty bitch Bernice. Tape postcard over hole.

Devil laughs. "The neighbors heard the shot. Now they'll call the cops. You'll have a whole lot of explaining to do."

He's not lying. Sirens shrill outside. Neighbor dogs howl.

"Here they come," Devil says.

Angel tells me, "Quick, hide behind the drapes."

Try to, but my rear end sticking out!

Siren zooms down street.

"Lucky you," Devil says.

Angel scolds, "You won't be so lucky next time."

Not feeling lucky. Smell smoke from gun. Grab perfume bottle, splash in front of closet. Perfume sticky on hands.

Go to living room. Plump Woman at window. "I thought I heard a car backfiring, then a siren raced down our street. Hope nothing bad happened."

"Dunno."

She steps close, too close. "Mom, you smell like you doused yourself with an entire bottle of perfume."

"Dunno."

Devil laughs. Kick him out of way.

Must tell Harry get rid of gun. Sit in Lazy-boy. "Wish Harry's here."

"I miss Daddy, too." Plump Woman sits beside me.

Black Snowball jumps onto lap, purrs loud.

Pet warm, soft fur. "Devil made me do it."

Mama says that's no excuse.

Say prayer Mama teaches me. "Now I lay me down to sleep and pray the Lord my soul to keep. If should die before awake . . ."

Don't know rest of prayer!

Tell Plump Woman, "Take me home, please!"

# Chapter 23 RIGHT ON TIME

Tell Gray Hair, "I'm good girl."

She listens to heart, knows it's true. Asks lots of silly things, has me draw three o'clock. My drawing so nice, she gives me lollipop.

Plump Woman and lady with dark hair squish into small room. Plump Woman sits by me. No chair for Dark Lady.

Gray Hair says, "Your mother is exhibiting a decline in cognitive ability. I would like to schedule her for more extensive tests."

Dark Lady blows out huge sigh. "She can't seem to remember things from one minute to the next, not unless it's from her childhood."

"Long term memories tend to stick with us more so than short term," Gray Hair says. "Have you observed any confusion or changes in her behavior?"

Plump Woman's voice breaks. "Everything is fine, then she does something erratic. I keep making excuses for her . . ." Sighs too, looks down.

Dark Lady sounds worried. "Is this Alzheimer's or dementia?"

Gray Hair folds hands. "I don't have enough information to make a diagnosis. Keep in mind that dementia describes a group of symptoms and that there are different types of dementia as well as multiple conditions that cause it. Alzheimer's is a disease with symptoms of dementia."

Why Plump Woman looking at me? She says, "What can we do?"

Hold out lollipop. She won't take lick.

Gray Hair says, "I would advise that you establish a routine at home and stick with it. Keep things simple and choose activities that don't require a lot of memory skill. A proper diet and safe environment are also essential. "

Plump Woman says. "I make nutritious meals but I can't get her interested in doing much of anything."

Dark Lady still worried. "Can you tell us anything about her prognosis?"

Proboscis? Know word! Means big nose. Mine too big?

Gray Hair looks at papers. "Her blood work is good and her vital signs are strong. Right now our main concern is to keep her safe and provide the best quality of life possible."

Plump Woman wipes her eyes. "I'm doing the best I can, but every day is a challenge."

"You can only do what you can do," Gray Hair says. "At this point you may not be able to reason with your mother, so try to focus on her feelings instead. Maybe give her small tasks that won't frustrate her."

"I'm afraid she's beyond that," Plump Woman says.

Gray Hair thinks. "You might try music to keep her engaged. It helps to leave the TV on."

Plump Woman says, "Mom isn't sleeping much." She turns red like cherries. "After Mom called 911, Adult Protective Services checked up on me."

Gray Hair says, "My nurse can give you a list of area agencies that offer adult services, including day care. If you want to continue to keep her at home, I suggest you bring in someone who can help with your mother and give you a break. Being a caregiver is an exhausting, full time job. You can easily wear yourself out."

Plump Woman stares at the floor. "We already brought in a lady to bathe and babysit her when I can go shopping. But Mom is at the point where she needs to be watched every minute of the day. Yesterday she almost burned the house down."

Uh-oh, naughty girl. Gray Hair might take lollipop away. Hang onto it with both hands.

Dark Lady says, "Putting Mom in a nursing home will be a financial hardship."

"We may have to rethink our options," Plump Woman tells her. "We can't have her endangering herself or anyone else."

Danger . . . danger . . . *Lost in Space* . . . robot waving arms . . .

Gray Hair says, "Only you can decide what's best but I'll give you the name of our city's Ombudsman. She can't recommend a specific nursing home but she can provide information to help you find one best suited to your mother's needs. If you do decide to put your mother in long term care, come and see me again. I will write her a medical order so she is eligible for Medicare or Medicaid."

Take lollipop out of mouth. "Take me home."

"She's always saying that," Plump Woman sighs. "I keep telling her she is home but it doesn't seem to help."

"Anxiety is a common manifestation," Gray Hair says. "She may be fixating on home as a safe place."

Plump Woman wipes eyes. "I wanted us to be close, but most of the time Mom acts like she doesn't know me."

Gray Hair sounds sad. "It feels like we lose our loved ones twice. First they leave us mentally, then physically."

Tears roll down Plump Woman's face. Gray Hair hands her pretty box filled with soft white paper. "You have to do the best you can, forgive yourself and move forward."

Jump up. "Take me home."

Plump Woman says, "Why don't we stop for pie and coffee, Mom?"

Dark Lady nods.

Nod too. "Home again home again, jiggity jig."

# **Chapter 24 ANOTHER TIME OUT**

Plump Woman and Dark Lady don't order cherry pie like me. Coffee helps them not get fat. Means more pie for me! Lick last cherry crumb from spoon. "So much better than what we get at home!"

Plump Woman shakes her head. "She insists on putting sugar on everything."

Dark Lady says, "Well, the lab tests show her blood levels are okay."

Run finger around edge of plate, lick wisp of whipped cream. "That's good—" Can't find word—slips off my tongue like buttered pea. "That's good fellow."

Plump Woman says, "We have a big problem on our hands and we need to come to a decision."

What? Hands look clean to me.

She tells Dark Lady. "I have to hide all the knives and scissors so Mom doesn't cut things up and I tie the refrigerator door shut because she keeps leaving it open. Yesterday she tried to flush a pair of rubber gloves down the toilet." Tears in eyes. "Mom, do you understand what the word *dangerous* means?"

"Dangerous . . . Rodney Dangerfield . . . dangerous . . . like dynamite." Smile, know answer!

Dark Lady stirs cream into coffee, clinks spoon against cup. "Mom, I'm afraid we can't keep you home any longer."

"House . . . home . . . home sweet home . . ." Smile at them. "Home sweet home. Take me home."

Plump Woman says, "It's not that simple."

Dark Woman sets coffee down. "I don't know how we're going to afford nursing care even if we sell the house."

"I know." Plump Woman reaches for cream. Pops open tiny carton. Cream splatters table. "Mom's only assets are the house and a couple of rings. That money will be gone in no time." Big sigh fills room. "I sure wish I could have made my living arrangement with her work out."

"I warned you it wouldn't be easy. You've been away for so long, you have no idea how difficult it's been for the last couple of years."

Plump Lady taps spoon against cup. "What do you want from me, Melissa? You want to hear me say you were right? Alright, I'll say it. Are you happy now?"

Dark Lady quiet.

Plump Woman talks. "I think we should call the Ombudsman and ask for help so we can figure out the best facility. I just wish you had managed her finances better."

Dark Lady frowns. "She's so stubborn, she wouldn't listen to me."

Plump woman meets Dark Lady's frown, makes hers deeper. "After all her money is spent she'll be on Medicaid. We'll have to pick up the tab if we want to keep her someplace decent."

"Don't look at me," Dark Lady says. "I'm paying rent and making car payments."

Plump Woman sounds upset. "I'm just saying we need to step up to the plate."

Why stepping on plates? "Ask Harry, he'll know what to do."

They shut up.

"More pie please?"

Plump Woman waves to our waitress and asks for more. She looks at me. "You know Mom, if you were in a nice home, you'd get pie every day."

"Home sweet home."

Dark Lady tilts nose in air. "I must say, Dawn, this is a 180 degree turn. When I suggested assisted living a while back you said I was a terrible daughter. But now you're fine with it."

Plump Woman red-nosed as reindeer. "Don't play that self-righteous card with me."

"Well, if the shoe fits—"

Mama's voice boils up inside me. "You girls stop bickering or I'll take you both home this very minute."

Dark Lady clams up.

Plump Woman goes bug-eyed then leans across table. "I know we've had our issues in the past, Melissa. But let's set that aside and think about Mom's needs." Takes my hand. "We love you, Mom. You know that, don't you?"

"Dunno."

Dark Lady says, "Now Mom, you know I love you and Dawn does, too."

Plump Woman nods. "We want what's best for you."

"Don't deserve best."

"Sure you do. We'll find a nice new place you can afford and where you'll be happy."

Sit up straight. Smile. "I'm baby. Everyone takes care of me." That's what Mama tells Sissy.

Two ladies look away.

Stuff cream cartons up coat sleeve for cats. White Snowball won't like cream but Black Snowball licks cream and purrs.

# Chapter 25 TIME AFTER TIME

Plump Woman sits in hubby Harry's chair. Looks like she ate something bad. Hope she doesn't throw up. "Mom, we need to talk."

"Okey dokey." Step far away.

Plump Woman clears throat. "Mom, I found a postcard taped over a hole in the closet door."

Shrug. "Mice make holes."

"This was five feet off the ground."

"Dunno."

"Our handyman says it looks like a bullet hole."

"Dunno."

"When Melissa and I were packing your clothes, we found Daddy's gun in your closet. One of the bullets is missing."

"Dunno."

"You need to be in a safer environment. You understand that, don't you?"

"Take me home."

"I can't do this anymore. Melissa can't, either. She's already used up all her vacation days and sick leave." Plump Woman starts cry. "We have no help. Edna quit after you hit her the last time she gave you a bath."

"Did not!"

"Yes, you did—" Plump Woman takes my hand, holds on tight. "I know you can't help it. I wish there was a cure but the doctor says—"

Pull hand back. "Everyone dies from something." Mama says that, too,

Plump woman looks upset. "I have to face facts. You need more care than I can give you."

Care? Care for baby girls! Look around. "Where's Dawn, Melissa?"

"I'm Dawn. Melissa's at work."

"Take me home."

Plump Woman says, "I'm sorry, Mom."

"About what?"

Deep breath. "I was hoping it wasn't too late to start over."

"Dunno." Go to window, soak up sunshine.

Plump Woman stares at floor. "Melissa and I found a place for you, one that we think you will like."

"Home, going home!" See Mama, Papa, Sissy.

Plump Woman raises hands, lets hands fall. "Since you and Daddy wouldn't consider assisted living earlier—"

Stand up. Black Snowball hops off my lap. "Can't afford it! Harry spending money on floozy."

"No he's not, Mom. Just calm down. Melissa and I checked with Social Services and we have a plan. After we sell your house and put all your money in your bank account, we'll use it so you can live in a place where you'll be safe."

"Want to go home."

She doesn't hear me.

"We want what's best for you, Mom."

Tears drip into my mouth, taste like salt. Pick up Black Snowball. "We go live with Sissy."

"Sissy passed away."

Passed away where? "Go live with Melissa."

"I'm afraid that won't work." Plump Woman pokes at phone, says, "Melissa, can you talk to Mom?"

Take phone. Hear baby girl's voice! "Melissa, that you?"

"Yes, Mom. We need you to understand that this is your best option. Dawn can't take care of you and I … You can't live with me because I have a one bedroom apartment and I work during the day."

Hand phone back, say, "Black Snowball and me want to live with Dawn."

Plump Woman says, "I'm Dawn, Mom. I've tried taking care of you but this isn't working out."

Starts cry. Put Black Snowball down, hug her.

She hugs me back.

# Chapter 26 THROUGH THE HOURGLASS

Flop onto flowered chair, watch Dark Lady and Plump Woman carry boxes.

Plump Woman says, "You'll have enough space in your new room for some of your favorite teapots from your collection, Mom."

"Dunno."

"Don't you want some of your treasures?"

Treasures! Treasure chest . . . Go to room, open drawer. Yes! Five heart shaped boxes. Open one. No chocolates.

Dark Lady comes in with a suitcase. "I found this in the basement. It's full of doll clothes." Holds up tiny dress for itsy bitsy people. "Just look at how intricate these ruffles are, Dawn."

Dawn . . . Dawn . . . Open and close eyes. Thinking Plump Woman sounds like my daughter Dawn.

I open and close my eyes, smile at my Plump Baby Girl Dawn.

Dawn smiles back, says, "You told us these were designer doll dresses that you ordered from Paris."

Turn the tiny dress inside out. "I didn't have money for doll clothes. I had to make dresses for you."

Dawn squeezes my hand. "We didn't appreciate the kind of time and effort you put into making these, did we Melissa?"

Melissa . . . Melissa . . . Open and close my eyes. Pretty Dark Hair Baby Girl Melissa!

She has tears in her eyes. "You made all our costumes for our dance recitals, too."

"Don't cry, Melissa. I'll make more costumes."

My Plump Baby Girl Dawn opens a drawer, takes out a large brown book. "Should we pack Mom's photo album?"

Dark Hair Baby Girl shakes her head. "I'll take it to my apartment for safe keeping." She looks at dresser drawers. "I'm so glad you're here, Dawn. This is hard, trying to decide what to pack for Mom to take with her."

Big sigh. Plump Baby Girl says, "Next we'll have to clear out the entire house."

Dark Hair Baby Girl says, "We could hire someone to hold an estate sale."

Stand up fast. "No, don't throw things away. Might need them later."

Dark Hair Baby Girl tells me, "You always say that but we can't keep everything, Mom."

Plump Baby Girl steps close. "Melissa, I know we've had our differences in the past but I want you to know that I'm here for the long haul." Gets quiet. "You're all the family I have left."

Nod quick. "Yes, yes! I'm the baby of the family. Everyone takes care of me." Even Sissy . . . Look around. "Where's Sissy?"

"She passed away, Mom," Dark Hair Baby Girl says.

"That Sissy! Always runs away, won't play with me."

My baby girls don't say anything.

# Chapter 27 TANGLED IN TIME

Plump Woman drives car, talks too fast. "This is a top notch facility, Mom. I'm sure you'll like it here." She parks by brick building. It's square and tall like a cereal box.

Dark Lady says. "This facility is second to none, Mom."

Building looks like school where my baby girls—

Gasp. "Dawn, Melissa! Where are they?"

Plump Woman asks, "What are you talking about?"

"My baby girls, Dawn and Melissa."

Dark Lady smiles. "That's us, Mom."

Laugh. "Yeah, right."

Plump Woman and Dark Lady take me into building. Nice inside. Blue, rose, lavender—smells like hotel.

Dark Lady goes up to main desk. "We have an appointment to see Mrs. Phillips."

Woman in blue clothes comes out, tells us, "This way, please."

Walk down long hallway with doors. Heart beats faster. Which door is Mama's garden?

Woman in Blue opens wrong door, goes into white room. Floor is color of hairballs that Black Snowball throws up. Stop in doorway, shake my head. "Wrong door."

Plump Woman says, "Now Mom, this may seem small but all you really need is a bedroom and bath. You'll be taking your meals in the main dining room."

Woman in Blue talks faster. "Our facility has an entertainment center where residents can watch movies and television on a big screen. We also schedule live entertainment weekly. Our mission is to maintain a comfortable, homey environment that offers the very best care for our residents."

This place full of old people. "Take me home." Step back into hallway. Throw open door—

"Hey!" Old man yells, pulls up pants.

"Sorry, we're so sorry." Plump Woman shuts door fast.

Dark Lady stops me. "Cool it, Mom. Don't make a scene."

Yep, old man without pants is obscene. "Take me home."

Plump Woman and Dark Lady look at each other.

Dark Lady clears throat. "This is your new home, Mom." Takes me back to small room.

Plump Woman gets photograph from dresser. "We brought a picture of you and Daddy."

"Mad at him."

"Now Mom—"

"Harry pays damn dirty bitch Bernice one thousand dollars to sleep with him. Never gave me one dime!"

Plump Woman hands me White Snowball. "Look, Mom, here's your toy cat."

"Want Black Snowball."

Dark Lady says, "I'm afraid you can't have pets here. But don't worry, Dawn is taking care of him."

"Take me home."

Plump Woman says, "Please, Mom, give this a chance."

What would Sissy do? Send letter to Papa! He'll take me home. Ask, "Need pencil and paper, please."

"Here you go, Mom." Plump Woman finds little book, pen in purse.

"Dear—"

How to write letter P? Pen goes round, around. In first grade we draw small circles inside big circles to make bunny rabbits.

Big-hip woman taps on door. "Mrs. Laska, it's time for dinner. Let me take you to the dining room."

Jumping Jehoshaphat, she makes me sit by old people. Should be at small table with kids my own age.

Stand up— Is that cherry pie? Sit down again. Pie for everyone! Gobble mine down. Old Lady says, "You shouldn't eat your dessert first."

Not my Mama. Can't tell me what to do.

Old Man at table eats dessert too. "This is what you call a monkey's lunch."

After we eat, Old Man walks me to room. Don't like having old geezer tag after pretty young girl like me. Toss my head, walk away. Mama says. "Old men just want a cook and a maid."

Clorox smell burns nose. Need roses from Mama's garden but first have to find the right door.

# Chapter 28 TEMPER TANTRUMS

Devil makes me do it. No, it's Old Lady's fault. She plops onto my flowery chair, won't budge. Tells me to find another seat.

Cross my arms. "This is my seat."

She looks down pointed nose. "First come, first serve."

Angel appears on my shoulder, shakes finger. "Little girls don't talk back to their elders."

Devil climbs onto other shoulder. "Bitchy old women don't count. Go ahead, pull her out of that chair."

Grab her arm. Feels soft and lumpy, like old bones covered with cobwebs. "Get the hell out of here!"

"Leave me alone!" Old Lady's scream hurts my ears.

Curly-haired man comes over. "What's going on?"

Point to Old Lady. "She took my chair."

Old Lady holds up arm. "She broke my wrist."

Arm is so wrinkled, who can tell?

"Let's find another chair, shall I?" Curly makes me sit on hard, leather seat.

Dig in my heels. "Want *my* chair."

Curly raises voice. "No one has their own chair around here. It's open seating."

Have to sit on the edge of hard seat. Wait until Old Lady moves . . .

Ah ha! Grab my flowery chair.

PRISON WARDEN COMES to my room with Plump Woman and Dark Lady.

Dark Lady says, "Mom, what were you thinking—picking a fight with another resident?"

"Dunno." Keep combing White Snowball. Silky fur falls out, sheds all over floor.

Prison Warden folds arms. "We take these altercations very seriously."

What alterations? "Clothes fit me fine."

Warden talks over my head. "Your mother is exhibiting severe mood swings and frequent memory lapses. We have no choice but to move her to a more secure facility that can address her special needs."

Hot diggity! Going home!

# Chapter 29 DÉJÀ VU ALL OVER AGAIN

Can't Dark Lady hear water roar? River rising! Grab her hand. "Run for high ground!" She stands stiff like statue. Big-hip Woman steps up. "It's alright, Mrs. Laska. That fountain in the lobby won't overflow and it won't hurt you." Closes door, tells Dark Lady, "She seems terribly afraid of water."

Nod quick. "Hate water."

Dark Lady says, "Especially baths."

Big-hip Woman tells her, "Our skin gets thinner as we age and we feel the cold more intensely." Hooks arm through mine. "Let's go back to your room, Mrs. Laska. You'll be safe there."

"Want to go home." Hold on tight. She's so big, water won't sweep us away.

Big-hip Woman goes down hallway, settles me on chair in small room.

"Don't leave me."

Dark Lady steps up. "I'm here, Mom. Dawn will be here soon."

"Goody." Dawn best time of day.

Big-hip Woman stops in doorway. "Is there anything I can get for you, Mrs. Laska?"

"Dunno."

Plump Woman knocks on door. She's Dark Lady's best friend. Want best friend, too!

"Hug?" Hold out arms. They hug me back.

"Look what I brought you, Mom." Plump Woman takes toy from bag. "Here's another White Snowball. You brushed your other one so much, the hair is falling out."

Fold arms. "Want Black Snowball."

"You don't have a kitchen and you know how much he likes to eat." Plump Woman picks up White Snowball. "This kitty won't eat anything."

Fold arms tighter. Want Black Snowball. He jumps like Monkey. Hold out arms. "Want to see Monkey."

"You mean you want to see the monkeys in the zoo?" Dark Lady asks.

Sissy has silly song. "Monkey in the sewing shop. Jumps on shelves with a hop, hop hop."

Plump Woman lowers her voice. "I did some research, Melissa. When Mom was a child, there was a sewing notions shop downtown that had a trained monkey. The store owner was in a wheelchair so the monkey fetched things for her off the shelves."

Dark Lady clears her throat. "That monkey moved to the zoo, Mom. We'll take you there next Tuesday. It's my day off."

Plump Woman nods. "It'll be fun, just the three of us like old times." She smiles at Dark Lady.

"Want to come too."

"Of course you will, Mom," Dark Lady says.

Smile. Sissy calls me tag-along sister. Best friends are okay with that.

# Chapter 30 CHANGING TIMES

Wake up at night dreaming Sissy and me play hopscotch on the playground. Bratty Boy across Street pushes me down—

Knees hurt.

Bratty Boy laughs.

Sissy sings, "Hey diddle diddle, cat with a fiddle. Can a cow jump over the moon?"

Man in Moon shines through window, laughs too.

Shake my fist at him. "Not funny." Go outside, look for Sissy.

Man with a moon-round face walks up to me. "Let's not wander the halls, Mrs. Laska."

Want to go home, find Mama's garden. "Help me find right door."

"Of course." Moon Face turns me in circle. "You poor dear, your knees are grating together. All the cartilage must be gone."

Cartridge? Christmas? Cartridge in pear tree?

Reach end of hallway. Small Man in Moon shines on wall. Face has numbers: nine, ten, eleven, twelve . . .

"Mama is waiting up for me."

All alone in small room. Get into bed, pull up covers over head.

Find hallway, open door—

Mama's rose garden! Laugh, dash up porch steps into house.

It's dark, so dark . . . Mama opens curtains first thing in morning, lets sunshine in. Why are windows shut tight?

"Mama?" Frightened, run from room to room. No one here. Hurry to backyard.

Other side of fence, kitten mews.

Open gate. Find baby cat in box. "It's all right, you're home now." Carry kitten inside.

Looks at me with pretty blue eyes. "You want milk—"

*Wizard of Oz* wind throws our house high into the air. "Help, Mama! Papa!" Hug kitten tight. Wind tosses our house higher.

House breaks into pieces like the glass ball that fell off our Christmas tree. It's Sissy's fault for chasing me.

Open eyes. "Kitty?" Run fingers over covers.

Tiny paws hurry down hallway . . . Kitty?

Swing legs from bed, stumble to door. Man in Moon shines on floor. Cold slaps feet.

Voice yells, "Mrs. Laska!" Footsteps loud behind me. Try to run but feet tangle in my old lady nightgown.

Thick legs fall to ground.

Someone turns off the Moon.

# Chapter 31 TIME SERVED

Voices . . . Hear my baby girls talking. Open my eyes.

Dawn says, "Mom, how do you feel?"

Close my eyes, open them. "Not hurt this bad since my baby girls were born." Try to sit up, can't move.

Hear Melissa say, "She seems more confused than ever since she fell."

Dawn sounds upset. "This is your fault."

Melissa says, "Why is it my fault?"

Dawn tells her, "You should have found a more secure facility."

Melissa sounds angry, "So says the armchair general who let me do all the leg work."

Dawn says, "Don't lay that guilt trip on me. I did my best, trying to take care of her."

Melissa crosses arms. "Oh really? You think you can just waltz back into her life and take control after being gone for years?"

Dawn says, "So sue me for trying to make up for lost time."

Melissa gets more upset. "Face it, you missed the boat. You should have moved back when Mom was still in her right mind."

Close eyes. Open eyes. My baby girls gone . . .

Plump Woman says, "Don't knock me for making the effort."

Dark Lady shrugs. "It was too little too late, Dawn. Mom doesn't know either of us anymore."

Search for voice, find it. "Girls!"

All quiet. Plump Woman says, "I'm sorry, Melissa. We shouldn't be squabbling, especially not in front of Mom."

Dark Lady frowns. "Well Dawn, I'm glad you're finally onboard."

"All we've got left is each other—unless Wayne proposes."

Sit up straight. "Wayne?"

Dark Lady shows me picture. "Wayne's the cowboy you met at your birthday party, Mom."

"Marry you?"

"No, Mom, he's my boyfriend."

Plump Woman says, "They're not getting married."

"Am I married?"

Dark Lady pats my hand. "No, Mom. Daddy passed away."

Shrug. "Do I have boyfriend?"

"I'm afraid not, Mom," Dark Lady says. "But you have us."

Plump Woman tells me, "I moved from California to be with you, Mom."

"Really?" Smile at Plump Woman, my New Best Friend.

Dark Lady and Plump Woman smile at each other, have a secret.

Want friends and secrets too!

# Chapter 32 FULL MOON LIKE THE MOON IN JUNE

Joy joy joy! My Plump Best Friend from California drives me to town. Sing Sissy's silly song, "We go to see the Monkey, Monkey, Monkey! Monkey lives in a sewing shop. Climbs on shelves with a hop hop hop."

My Plump Best Friend looks sad. "That shop went out of business years ago, Mom, but you might remember the candy store next to it. You took Melissa and me there all the time when we were kids. We liked to watch the mechanical doll in the window pulling saltwater taffy."

"Dunno."

My Plump Best Friend parks in front of a building by a big glass window. We watch a boy doll with a tall white hat turn a crank, stretch a long piece of candy. Pull and fold, pull and fold—

My Plump Best Friend takes my hand. We go inside.

She talks to White Hair Lady in store. "I'm glad your mechanical doll is still functioning."

White Hair Lady says, "That little guy is barely moving these days, just like me."

My Plump Best Friend tells White Hair Lady, "I'm Dawn Laska. My sister Melissa and I used to come in all the time before I moved to California. I'm so glad you're still here."

White Hair Lady says. "I've been behind this same counter for years. I took over the shop when my parents retired." Looks at My Plump Best Friend, looks at me. "Now I recognize your mother. It's been a while."

Gives me a hug, don't know why.

Plump Woman smiles big. "Mom's got a sweet tooth. That's why we're here. "

Smile and nod. Candy on shelves everywhere.

My Plump Best Friend asks, "What would you like, Mom?"

Open arms. "Want everything."

See yellow monkey on counter holding sign. "Try our new banana flavor."

Clap hands. "Monkey! Want Monkey!"

My Plump Best Friend asks White Hair Lady, "Would you be willing to sell that toy monkey?"

White Hair Lady says, "That's a display piece. All the kids love it. I'm sorry, but it's not for sale."

My Plump Best Friend says, "I'll be glad to pay you for it. It would mean so much to my mom. One of the few happy things she remembers is your candy store and the sewing notion shop next door. Apparently the owner was disabled and had a trained monkey that climbed on the shelves to fetch things for her."

White Hair Lady nods. "I remember that little monkey, too. It sure kept children entertained while their mothers shopped." Looks at me funny.

Hold out my hands. "Love Monkey."

White Hair Lady thinks, hands Monkey to me. "I believe this little fellow does need a new home."

Hug him tight.

"Thank you, thank you." Plump Best Friend says, buys four boxes of fudge.

White Hair Lady smiles wide. "When I'm her age, I hope my daughter cares about me this much."

We leave candy store. My Plump Best Friend pats her tummy. "Sure don't need these extra calories."

Monkey and me stop, stare. "Why? You so beautiful."

Plump Best Friend gets tears. "Thanks, Mom, I've been waiting to hear that all of my life." Opens car door.

My Plump Best Friend drives car. Monkey and me watch fuzzy clouds in sky.

Back in small room, Dark Hair Friend waits for us. She tells My Plump Best Friend, "This fudge from the Candy Corner is so delicious, I could eat the whole box."

My Plump Best Friend sits me and Monkey on chair by window.

Dark Hair Friend opens box, hands me candy.

Smells good so ask, "Do I like this?"

"Yes, Mom, fudge is your favorite."

Tastes sweet. "Damn good baloney."

Plump Best Friend laughs, eats piece too.

Dark Hair Friend smiles. "Remember my tenth birthday, Mom?"

"Dunno."

"We had a terrible snowstorm and none of the girls I invited could come. Daddy was working so there was just you, me and Dawn. You set all our dolls around the table and we had our own little party. I remember that year I got roller skates and we all had big slices of cake. Then we played the Candy Land game a million times." Squeezes my hand. "Thank you, Mom. I love you."

Mouth full, give her chocolate kiss. Kiss My Plump Best Friend too.

They kiss me back. My Plump Best Friend says, "I'm sorry we can't do better for you, Mom. This isn't the nursing home we preferred, but it's all we can afford between your social security and what Melissa and I can pitch in—"

Pitch . . . Papa pitches balls at carnival, wins Cupie doll. "Mama's waiting up for me." Ask My New Best Friends, "Take me home."

"You are home, Mom."

Home . . . look for home out window. Only see clouds floating on blue like water blue—breaking through sky ceiling!

Grab Monkey, run to door.

My Plump Best Friend says, "Where are you going, Mom?"

"Monkey scared."

Dark Hair Friend hugs me. "It's alright, Mom. We're here."

# Chapter 33 TIME FLOWS ON AND ON AND ON

My Plump Best Friend drives me and Monkey to have ice cream with Dark Hair Friend. We go back to my hotel room.

"Sun so bright!" Wear my special occasion hat with pink roses.

My Plump Best Friend says, "Let's take off your coat, Mom."

Wearing clothes under my coat? Scared to look. Tell My Friends, "Don't have any clothes!"

Dark Hair Friend goes to a door, opens it. "Look at this, Mom, you have a closet full of clothes." Counts: one, two, three . . . ten . . . twenty—all good numbers.

Sit on chair by window. Scared again. "Don't have any clothes!"

"Now, Mom, you have lots of clothes." She goes to a door, opens it. Counts: one, two, three . . . ten . . . twenty. "See, you have a lot of outfits."

Sit by window, watch pink clouds that look like cotton candy. Feeling sleepy, hum Mama's song.

Plump Best Friend says, "You used to sing that lullaby to Melissa and me when we were little."

Dark Hair Friend sings in her sweet voice, "Rock-a-bye, don't you cry. Day will break by and by. Birds are singing in the sky. Spread your wings and learn to fly."

Song flutters like the blue jays in Mama's garden. My Beautiful Best Friends sing like angels.

Sun sets fire to clouds. Moon floats like a white balloon in dark sky.

Take deep breath. My Plump Best Friend wears camellia perfume like Mama wears on Sundays. "So glad we're best friends."

"I am too, Mom."

"We're best friends like me and Sissy." Look everywhere. "Where's Sissy?"

"She passed away, Mom."

"Again? She does that a lot."

Dark Hair Friend says, "Yes, Mom, she certainly does."

My Plump Best Friend puts her hand on my shoulder.

We watch sky go black. My Plump New Friend says, "You know, Mom, there were times when I wished I had a child." Brushes my hair. "Sometimes you make me feel like I have one."

"Dunno."

Lean close, smell sweet camellias. Only wear perfume on Sunday along with my best dress. Turn to Dark Hair Friend, "So afraid. Don't have any clothes."

Dark Hair Friend says, "You have a closet full of clothes, Mom."

"Want to go home."

My Plump Best Friend says, "Let's hope that Alexa device I ordered is still connected to the facility's Wi-Fi." She fiddles with small box on my dresser.

Dark Hair Friend sighs. "It drives me crazy when Mom repeats herself."

"She can't help it," My Plump Best Friend says.

"I know that but—" Dark Hair Friend acts like tiny person lives inside box. "Did you program that default wake phrase for Alexa?"

My Plump Best Friend nods. "Yes, let's see if it works."

"Want to go home," I say.

Tiny person inside box talks to me. She has nice voice. "You are home."

Dark Hair Friend says, "Thank heavens for inventions."

Wait for this tiny person to pop out like Jack-in-the-box. Tell Voice-in-the-box, "Want to go home."

Nice voice says, "You are home."

"Want to go home."

"You are home."

"Want to go home."

My Plump New Friend from California stands up, kisses me. "I'll see you tomorrow, Mom."

Dark Hair Friend kisses me too. "Alexa will keep you company while we're gone."

Alexa. New tiny friend with nice voice inside box is Alexa.

My Plump New Friend hugs Dark Hair Friend. They go out the door together.

Fold my arms, tell Alexa, "Want to go home."

"You are home."

We talk all night.

Dawn comes. Alexa still talking.

FROM THE AUTHOR:

This story is not biographical but I did include some of my mother's witticisms as she developed Alzheimer's. No manuscript is completed without assistance and I am grateful to my friend and writing partner Alice Hill for editing as well as Becky Espinoza and Judy Arko who contributed ideas and insights to the story line.

With the percentage of elderly patients suffering from Alzheimer's and other forms of dementia on the rise, many women find themselves thrust almost overnight into the role of caretaker. Education is critical, and The I Will Projects, a 501-c3 nonprofit of which I am president (theiwillprojects.com) has sponsored a course in partnership with Hospice to train and inform nurses and caregivers in palliative care.

Alzheimer's is a thief of the mind but there's a glimmer of hope. Although it does disintegrate relationships, it can also create new ones. There are plateaus that feel manageable and become a new normal. When your loved one deteriorates, it's only natural to second guess if you've made the right decisions. Guilt and regret can and do arise, but please realize that in the end all that can be expected is that you use your best judgment and do what you can in any given situation.

Although it's easy to become mired in the tedium of Alzheimer's, there are takeaways worth noting. One is a renewed appreciation of the person you are caring for and an awareness of the limited time allotted to you. Another is a reminder that we rely on each other for support, so never wait too long to make your peace with someone you cherish.

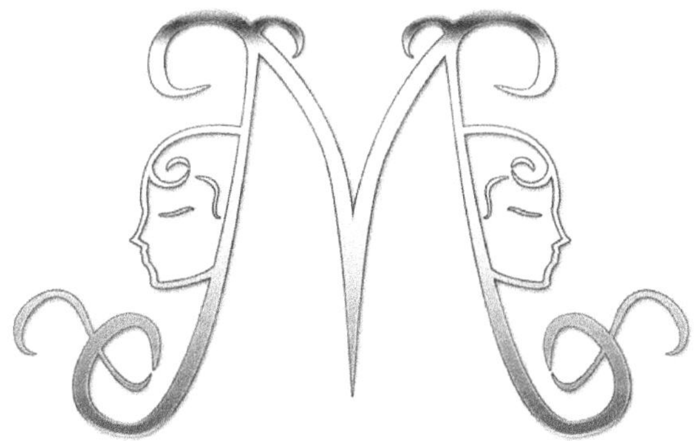

## About the Author

Marlene Fabian Stiles began to write before she could write, dictating stories to her mother at the age of 5. She and her mother became best friends but as Alzheimer's set in, her mother also became both the child and the sister she never had.

Read more at www.storystyles.com.